WHAT
THE
Wealth?!

A GUIDE TO
FINANCIAL CLARITY
FOR PROFESSIONALS AND FAMILIES

JONATHAN P. BEDNAR, II, CFP®
CERTIFIED FINANCIAL PLANNER™

Published in the United States by Jonathan P. Bednar, CFP®.

Bednar, II Jonathan P.

What the Wealth?!

A Guide to Financial Clarity for Professionals and Families / Jonathan P. Bednar, II

ISBN #978-0-578-59831-4

Edited by: Candice Elliott, Sandy Bakke and Fran Linardo

Graphic Design by: Carley Beyer

Printed in the United States of America

Dedication

What The Wealth?! A Guide to Financial Clarity for Professionals and Families is dedicated to my Daughter Catherine Elizabeth. You are just a toddler now and won't be facing these challenges for many years, but I wanted to make sure that you always had a resource that helps you understand the basic concepts of money and acts as a guide for your future.

Cate, I am incredibly proud to be your dad and I know your mom is as well. You will never know how much we love you. Even at such a young age we can see your caring heart. My advice to you:

Lean on the Lord to guide you. Pray for Wisdom!

Lean on your Family and Friends. Ask for support!

Life is full of trials and tribulations. Never Give Up!

Life Is short. Invest in your happiness!

Time is not supposed to be spent. It is to be invested. Always pursue your passions!

If you don't know where you are going, then any road will get you there. Be intentional and have a plan!

I'll love you forever! – Dad

Table of Contents

Introduction

Having a financial plan is an important practice for everyone. A plan outlines financial goals and shows step-by-step what can be done to reach those goals. The right strategy will seek to provide family security both now and in the future.

Personal finance can be intimidating and covers many aspects. Some aspects, investing in particular, can seem like a foreign language. Therefore, I'm going to address each part of financial planning chapter-by-chapter. Each chapter will cover a different phase of personal finance. Proceeding step-by-step through the chapters will provide an easy-to-follow plan, along with a few great tools, to help build an individualized financial plan.

I know that personal finance isn't exactly the sexiest or most entertaining subject; however, I will try to make what many consider to be a dry subject, entertaining and interesting. Whether or not I'm successful will be up to the reader to decide.

Many Americans lack a personal finance education. If a school addresses finance at all, it's usually cursory. In today's culture many consider money issues taboo; therefore, families don't talk about finance. If personal finance has not been addressed in the educational system and not within the family, mistakes will happen all too frequently (like drowning in credit card debt or waiting too long to invest). Some, out of fear, never invest at all.

Without financial knowledge, vulnerability to predators (like payday lenders or unscrupulous financial advisors) grows exponentially. Perhaps more than any subject (apart from health), personal finance will have the most impact on the quality of life experienced.

Over the course of my career, I have helped hundreds of people improve their financial situations. Sometimes I've had to help them climb out of a deep financial hole. A few basic pieces of personal finance knowledge would have helped them avoid these problems.

Sometimes these situations frustrated and angered me. I wasn't angry with my clients; I was angry with their problem. As I stated before, if not taught how to handle money at school or home, it's easy to wind up in a bad situation. I wanted to help more people outside the scope of my job. Although I am very dedicated, I can only speak with a limited amount of people each day. Due to this personal experience, I decided to write this book.

I want this book to help people who will never walk into my office. I want this to help people who know very little about personal finance or planning. I want those who do understand finance to come away with a little more understanding.

Chapter One:

The "B" Word – Budgeting

The first and most important step of financial planning is creating a budget. The second is sticking to a budget. I'll show how to do both.

Budgeting, practically a curse word in some homes, is a task that everyone loves to hate. Budgeting can seem cumbersome, time-consuming, and exhausting; however, budgeting allows the creation of an optimal plan to pursue personal goals and passions. In my opinion, traditional budgets do not work. Usually, life gets in the way. Let's be honest, there is nothing sexy about a budget unless one happens to be a finance nerd. In my household, my wife is the budgeter.

The reason that traditional budgeting does not work is that many budgets are too reactionary. They tend to look at what happened in retrospect. A typical monthly budget has categorized allocated spending. When reconciled at the end of the month, the planned budget usually shows overspending or underspending in one or more categories. However, overspending behavior is not addressed. Having a budget does not prevent overspending.

The same applies to online budgeting tools. They do a great job at tracking spending, but they usually do a poor job of changing spending behavior. This doesn't mean you should fail to understand how the money "soldiers" are working. Where your money goes is quite important. I recommend two styles of budgeting: the envelope system and the zero-based budget system. I will discuss both options and provide examples.

Everyone Needs a Budget

Just as some people think financial planning is only for wealthy people, some think having a budget is only for poor people. This is simply false. Everyone needs a budget no matter how much or how little money is involved.

Although you might have a "rough" idea of how much money is coming in and how much is going out, a "rough" idea isn't good enough. You wouldn't accept a job offer if you only had a "rough" idea of what salary you would be earning, would you? Quite likely there are areas of life where you're spending more than you realize. A budget will help identify these.

Budgeting Systems

Using credit cards carry certain advantages. These include fraud and consumer protections that cash cannot provide. If something were to happen to the cash, it's gone with no recourse for recovery. If your debit/credit card is lost or stolen, you report it to the bank and then they take care of the problem.

For some of us, swiping a debit or credit card doesn't feel like spending "real" money. It's not tangible the way paper money is. This can sometimes lead to trouble. Your budget for eating out might be $100 a month, but your credit card limit is much higher. You can see how this could be problematic. If that sounds familiar, then you may want to try the old school cash envelope system, not the most efficient way to budget, but highly effective. If the many options you've tried have all failed, this might be the one that works best for you. If you want to use the envelope system but prefer digital tools, there is a tool for that which I'll cover later.

The Envelope System

1. Take a snapshot of your current financial position, meaning how much you earn each month.

2. List your spending categories. These are usually broken down into non-discretionary expenses (rent/mortgage, utilities, groceries, debt, et cetera) and discretionary expenses (gym membership, restaurants, travel, et cetra).

3. Take your monthly income and assign a part of that into each category using the 50/30/20 budgeting method detailed below.

4. As you spend money, take it out of the corresponding envelope. Once that envelope is depleted, stop spending in that category.

5. Replenish the envelopes each month.

You may have money leftover in a category. These funds will help you build a reserve. In ours, we have a "car maintenance" envelope. This money is set aside to cover necessities like oil changes, brake pads, or new tires. These are not crises (meaning we won't use the emergency fund), but they are not monthly expenses either. This category will build up as we contribute regularly to it. When new tires are needed, the funds will be there waiting inside the car maintenance envelope. This will help change spending behavior, as it allows you to visualize the concept.

Zero-Based Budgeting

The second budgeting system I recommend is a "Zero-Based Budget". This method earmarks all your money for specific expenses until you get to zero. Each part of your income is given a job. All expenses must be justified each month or pay period. You should pay yourself first; then add savings, investments, and rainy-day fund. If you do not have an emergency fund, add this as a line-item to build up six to nine months' worth of living expenses.

Assume you make $4,000 a month; put this at the top under income. As you work your way down, you will assign money from your income into the various expense categories. Typically, you should start with your most important and non-discretionary expenses. It is possible to run out of money before you have paid all your bills. If that's the case, you should identify where you can trim back to pay all your expenses.

Budgeting Tools

Goodbudget and *MVelopes* are two online services created to help you build an envelope-style budget. These come in a desktop version and mobile app. Goodbudget offers a free version including twenty envelopes. You can sync the account containing those envelopes across two devices. If you want the ability to sync more devices, create more envelopes, and have unlimited accounts; you would need to use their paid version. The paid version is inexpensive (as of 2019 the paid version is $6 per month). The downside to Goodbudget is that it does not integrate with banks or credit cards. This means one must manually record transactions as they occur. The user interface is also a bit archaic, but straightforward. Sometimes less is more and the simplicity of Goodbudgets is appealing.

Mvelopes is a more modern approach to the envelope system. The layout and user interface are much more desirable than Goodbudget. Not only does Mvelopes help create a budget, but it also offers features such as debt-reduction strategies. It covers the "debt snowball" or "debt avalanche" methods, which we will discuss in chapter three. The software shows envelope balances while comparing spending, funding, and budget.

A useful feature of Mvelopes is the ability to link bank accounts, credit cards, student loans, et cetra. This allows you to sync transactions, so you do not have to manually input each. Mvelopes offers a smart categorization feature that automatically places repeated transactions in the correct category, a major time saver.

The downside is that they do not offer a free version of the software. They provide a 30-day free trial. After that, you must select the "basic", the "plus", or the "complete". This might be worthwhile to avoid manually inputting every single transaction, which might increase the likelihood of sticking with the budget.

The next two tools are based on zero-based budgeting. These are *EveryDollar* and *You Need A Budget (YNAB)*. If you have irregular income, I suggest using one of these options to put in place a zero-based budget.

EveryDollar is a budgeting program by Dave Ramsey, the no-nonsense budgeting and debt elimination coach. His experienced advice has helped millions of people become debt-free and build emergency funds while gaining confidence with money management.

EveryDollar offers a basic and paid version. The paid version allows you to connect your bank accounts and allows transactions to auto-populate within the app. Although the paid version saves time, I know many people who have no problem using the free version to manually record their transactions. You can also use this app to help track your debt elimination strategy.

The EveryDollar platform has a great user interface and is easy to use. The only drawback is that you cannot link credit cards due to Dave Ramsey's anti-debt stance. You will have to manually record credit card transactions.

YNAB uses zero-based budgeting which means you assign each dollar a task (paying a bill, paying down debt, investing for retirement, et cetra). There is no "leftover" money at the end of each month because each dollar is assigned a specific task. This is helpful for those who have trouble staying on a budget.

For those with inconsistent income, YNAB is a great budgeting system. It uses last month's income, which is a known quantity, to pay for the following month's expenses. It can take a few months for the numbers to work if you're currently living paycheck to paycheck. However, by carefully using the program as intended, you'll get there. This system is designed to end the practice of depending on the money you haven't yet earned to pay your bills.

Setting up your profile is straight-forward. Just link your accounts to the program and the information is synchronized. You can set up budget categories using default values or create your own. Next, you'll create the accounts from which you spend money (checking, savings, and credit cards).

Now you'll budget your money. Remember, this is zero-based budgeting, so your goal is to see $0 under "Available to Budget." Lastly, you'll record your spending. Whether you can spend money depends not on how much is in your accounts but on how much you've budgeted. If you bring in more than you've budgeted, you'll need to decide where to save it, not spend it.

YNAB has a steeper learning curve than other budgeting programs, but it is a good solution if you've failed at budgeting in the past. YNAB pretty much has a cult-following in personal finance circles. If you need help or advice, there are forums within the community to assist you. There are even tutorials for when you run into problems or have questions.

If you prefer a more traditional method of budgeting designed to track your spending, Mint is a good option. Mint is free and quite easy to use. Upon creating your account, you can provide information for things such as bank accounts, credit cards, loans, or investments. Mint will then automatically sync this info with your account.

Each time you log into your account, your information is refreshed. From your dashboard, you'll be able to see a summary of your personal finances. You can also provide your Social Security number to get a free credit score from Mint (after answering a few verification questions). We are going to talk more about credit scores in chapter eight.

Mint will automatically categorize each downloaded transaction into pre-set categories. You can create subcategories within your Mint account but cannot change the primary ones. This automatic categorization is not always ideal; however, you can manually move transactions.

You can also enter transactions manually. This comes in handy for cash transactions and other expenditures which may not be tracked by Mint. You will still have to remember where and on what you spent your cash.

Mint will download the last few months of transactions. Before you create a budget, go through these transactions to see where you've spent more than you realized you were spending. Most of us think along the lines of eating out as an easy place to overspend. However, for those who are gift givers that might just be where you are overspending.

On the Overview page, you can see the account balances for all connected accounts.

Mint allows you to create a budget by setting spending limits for each category. You can set alerts to notify you when you're getting near a budget category limit. The app can remind you of bills due. This information updates in real-time. You can also budget for non-monthly expenses, like property taxes. This helps you set a bit of money aside each month to pay for large, infrequent expenses.

Mint also allows you to track goals: saving for a vacation or an emergency fund. You can build savings for these goals into your monthly budget. If you have surplus money at the end of the month, Mint encourages you to use that money to help reach your goal.

The 50/30/20 Budget

Now that you've chosen a budgeting program, you need a budgeting method. There are plenty to choose from, but I like to keep things simple. That's why I like the 50/30/20 budget. It works the same for everyone no matter how much money they earn.

You will need to know how much your net income (after taxes) is each month. This includes all sources of income: your job, a side-hustle, alimony, et cetra. On this number you'll base your budget.

Computing this number is harder for those who have a variable income. If this describes your situation, look back over the last few months and use your average minimum monthly income. You do not want to use average monthly income because this may overestimate reality. You may experience months in which your income decreases from the average, so use the minimum and then you won't be overestimating.

Using your minimum might require you to make some sacrifices, but it is better than coming up short. Once you have your net income number, you are finally ready to budget.

Half of your income (50%) is budgeted for your essential living expenses. This includes things like housing, utilities, car payments, and insurance. Most of these expenses are fixed, meaning they don't vary from month-to-month. Ideally, you should keep your housing payment at-or-below 30%. Anything more than 30% puts you at risk of living paycheck-to-paycheck.

30% of your income is for discretionary spending. This is money budgeted for the more enjoyable things in life: clothes, shoes, golf, books, vacations, dinner out, gifts, or whatever else you enjoy.

20% of your income is for the "grown-up" stuff. This includes paying off debt, investing, saving for a home, a child's education, or retirement.

If you have high-interest debt (credit card or payday loans), consider devoting 30% of your budget to this. Then dedicate 20% to discretionary spending. This requires some painful spending cuts, but high-interest debt is an anchor on your financial planning goals.

If you are getting a late start on investing, you might want to consider this strategy. The most important component of investing is not how much money you have; it's how long that money is invested. If you need to make up for lost time, investing an additional 10% can help you do so.

Your money may not magically fit into this formula. If that's the case, you'll have some decisions to make. You either need to cut your spending or increase your income, ideally both.

Creating Budget Categories

If you have trouble sticking with a budget, you can use broad categories when setting it up (rent/mortgage, car, entertainment, etc… You need to expand your categories if you frequently go over budget by having a "black hole" into which money is vanishing or money is disappearing in a certain category.

An example would be "entertainment." Rather than using such a broad category, you could break it down into more specific subcategories:

- Cable

- Streaming & Subscription services

- Books

- Movies

- Concert tickets

Breaking down your categories can help you pinpoint spending issues that we all have.

Budgeting for Large Expenses

We all face large expenses. Sometimes we know they're coming and sometimes they're unexpected. The unexpected expenses are the reason why you should develop an emergency fund. We're going to cover this in-depth in chapter two.

Expected expenses still have a way of sneaking up on us, even though they're expected. Thus, we run around each year trying to buy a Mother's Day gift on Mother's Day.

When you are setting up your budget, look at the past twelve months: list annual expenses such as property taxes, renter's insurance premiums, tax preparation fees, or membership dues; next divide the cost by the number of months necessary to save for these expenses (usually twelve months); finally, factor those amounts into the monthly budget. This way you're more prepared for the next twelve months and won't be surprised by expected but forgotten expenses.

If you have a good credit score, there is another way to budget for large expenses. You can apply for a credit card with a 0% APR introductory period. Check out Credit Karma, both for your free credit score and credit card recommendations. The 0% period can range from 6 months all the way up to 24 months (although those are hard to find). Look for the card with the longest introductory period.

If you're approved, you can charge a large expense to this card. If you pay this off in full before the introductory period ends, you won't pay a penny in interest. The credit card has basically acted as a personal loan with 0% interest. Again, this trick only works if you pay off the card in full before the APR changes. If you can, then you've succeeded in spreading out the expenditure. Buyer beware! If you do not pay the balance off in full before the introductory term is over then the credit card company will charge interest on the entire amount financed. I do not recommend this strategy.

Budgeting for Life Changes

A budget is not a static practice. You don't sit down when you're eighteen, create a budget and never think about it again. Life changes and your budget must change with it. In fact, every year brings change and every year the budget needs to be reviewed.

We can't always predict life changes and their costs, but there are ways to "ballpark" any situation.

If you're moving to a new city, you can use a cost of living comparison calculator to evaluate the costs. If you are moving, you're presumably changing jobs as well. You can use sites like

Glassdoor, Salary.com, or PayScale to see what your position pays in other areas.

If you are moving in with your partner or getting married, you (hopefully) have an idea of his or her finances. This will give you an idea of how your household income and expenses will change.

If you're planning on having a child, there is plenty of data on how much it costs across a variety of circumstances. On average, it costs about $234,000 to raise two children to age 18. From birth to age two, the average yearly cost is about $13,000. There you have it, a "ballpark" figure. If you want to have a baby, start looking for an extra $13,000 each year.

Of course, big life changes happen to all of us. Whether we are prepared or not, we somehow make it work. With so much information available to us, you should consider how these changes will affect your budget. We need to make sure a big change doesn't cause a significant problem when personal finances are concerned.

Several years ago I had a client, Megan, who relocated for her job. She was excited for the new opportunity and advancement inside the company, as well as the move to a new city to explore. After the "newness" of the city and new job wore off she realized she wasn't as happy as she thought she would be and was becoming lonely. Far from her friends and family, Megan realized that being closer to them was becoming increasingly more important to her. I recommended she not rush into making quick decisions but to give the new city and job another sixty days. Usually making a hurried decision is the wrong decision because it is influenced too much by emotions and not enough by a well thought out plan. After the sixty day was over, Megan decided moving nearer to where she grew up and to where she had friends and family would provide a more fulfilling life. For her, spending time with those she cared about outweighed the excitement of the city. Megan had been a good budgeter and saver. She had amassed a nine month emergency fund, so she had the financial ability to take the leap and move closer to home.

Even though this wasn't a true emergency having this fund allowed her the flexibility to move back and support herself while she found a new job in the area without settling for the first offer.

Megan's story, though simple, illustrates the importance of having a budget and acquiring and keeping an emergency fund just in case you find you're without a job, whether due to a move or a true emergency. The following chapter discusses just what an emergency fund is and how to acquire the needed money to establish one.

Chapter Two:

Emergency Fund

An emergency fund is one of the most important tools in your financial plan. I'll explain what an emergency fund is, where to stash it, how much it should contain, and how you can build one. According to a recent study by the Federal Reserve[1], four in ten adults are unable to cover an unexpected expense of $400.

Several years ago, I had a client, whom we'll call Mike, diagnosed with a rare disease that required surgery and a few days in the ICU. Once discharged recovery at home lasted another 30 days. Since he was self-employed, the family was without income during that period. Luckily they had planned ahead and were able to access savings stored in the emergency fund to cover those out-of-pocket medical and living expenses.

---

[1] *https://www.federalreserve.gov/publications/files/2017-report-economic-well-being-us-households-201805.pdf*

What is an Emergency Fund?

An emergency fund is cash set aside for unexpected, essential expenses. Having an emergency fund can insulate your life from a devastating financial setback. It can take years to build an adequate fund; but it's one of the most critical parts of financial planning.

Only use your emergency fund under very specific circumstances. It's not meant to be fun money. Many years might pass without the necessity of having to dip into your emergency fund, but it's there should you need it.

Your emergency fund will not have enough to cover every monthly expense; only the vital ones (housing, utilities, insurance, food, et cetera) should be included when deciding on how much to put aside.

What Qualifies as an Emergency?

Unless your luck is particularly rotten, you should not find yourself in a financial emergency often. An example of a financial emergency could include a car repair (which could prevent you from getting to work), refrigerator replacement, or period of unemployment.

An emergency is not: a TV for the bedroom, a trip to Vegas, or a Rolex. An emergency is a need, not a want, and you should not touch your reserve fund unless you must.

How Much Do You Need in Your Emergency Fund?

Read it and weep — the ultimate emergency fund contains enough to cover six to nine months of expenses. But you can relax, this does not include all expenses and you can build your fund steadily.

The first step is to accumulate $1,000. This is an urgent priority. You can take a bit of time to build up a full-fledged fund, but you need to start with this amount.

Once you have the first thousand, start accumulating reserves in three-month intervals. Remember, it doesn't need to be enough to cover all your current monthly expenses. Imagine you lost your job. Which unnecessary expenses could you cut out of your life?

- Cable
- Dining out
- Retirement contributions
- Monthly investing
- Entertainment
- Clothing
- Subscription services
- Lawn care
- House cleaner
- Childcare

Also consider the expenses for which you would be responsible:

- Housing

- Utilities

- Insurance

- Car payments

- Medications

- Groceries

- Debt repayments

When saving for your emergency fund (especially the first $1,000), try to cut non-essential expenses like subscription services or eating out. You don't have to live without this forever but cutting back for a month or two can help you progress quicker. Another way to quickly build up the first $1,000 emergency fund is to sell items you no longer use.

The purpose of this fund is to be prepared for life's unexpected events. By having an adequate backup plan, you can reduce stress and anxiety centered around money. You need to become laser-focused on building a rainy-day nest egg. To do that, it may be beneficial to suspend some of your investment contributions. Ideally, this will be for a very short time. The exception is your 401(k). I do not recommend suspending your 401(k) contributions. You should be contributing enough to get the full employer match (more on this later). Once your emergency fund is built and debt (assuming you have debt) is paid, you can resume investing.

I discovered two tools that can help you cut expenses with minimal effort. The first is Trim. This service will sort through your monthly expenses and find recurring ones. Trim finds subscription services such as meal delivery kits, makeup boxes, or streaming services and gives you the option to cancel them. This is free of charge.

Secondly, Billshark will negotiate better rates for services such as cable, mobile, internet, satellite radio, or home alarm systems. Simply give them your account information and they do the rest. Many of these subscriptions have special offers and incentives to keep current customers. Most people do not take the time to research and haggle while trying to take advantage of these offers. Billshark does the hard part for you.

While you're looking for ways to save money, you should also look for ways to make more money. The internet and smartphones have made this easier than ever. Many ways exist to generate extra income. The "sharing" economy has enabled people to find flexible work at competitive rates.

Consider renting out your home for a few weekends on home-sharing sites like Airbnb and VRBO (Vacation Rentals Buy Owner). Drive for a ride-sharing service like Uber or Lyft. Postmates and Uber Eats are attractive options for less-social people. Perform odd jobs through Task Rabbit. Pet sit or babysit through Care.com and Rover.com. Check out freelancing sites like Upwork or Guru. These call for a wide range of trades such as writing, web design, or graphic arts.

Here are three great "side hustles" you might not have heard of:

1. VIPKid – Teach children in China the English language. You set your schedule, allowing you to teach where and when you want.

2. Rover – Do you like animals? This company connects you with people who need a pet-sitter and allows you to set your fees/ hours.

3. Instacart – Many people loathe the idea of going to the grocery store. What if you could get paid to do the grocery shopping and delivery for them?

*Note – I am not affiliated with any of these companies and do not earn a referral fee from them.

When you run into extra money from a raise, a bonus, a tax refund, or a monetary gift, stash it in your emergency fund. Saving up nine months of basic expenses can seem like a tall order but doing so is worth the sacrifice. An emergency fund can provide a great deal of confidence. Knowing that you can handle financial setbacks that we all face is a powerful thing.

Where to Keep Your Emergency Fund

An emergency can arise at any moment. Your fund needs to be liquid, meaning you can access it quickly (if not instantly). The most obvious choice is your checking account. If you're not a disciplined spender, that can be a problem. Inflation can also erode your checking account over time. Having extra money sit with your "regular" money might be too tempting for some people.

A savings account is a better choice. You can still readily access the money, but it's separated from your operating cash. This solution is okay when your emergency fund contains $1,000 or three months of expenses. In the scheme of things, that isn't much money.

But when you work up to six and nine months, that's a large amount of money to be sitting in a savings account earning less than 1% interest. In fact, your money isn't even keeping up with inflation in most cases.

A few alternatives offer better returns than a standard savings account. Online banks with no brick and mortar locations offer a more competitive rate than most traditional banks. A money market account allows you to write checks from it, but many have a minimum balance requirement such as $2,500. Should the balance fall below that, a fee may be charged. A CD (certificate of deposit) does not allow you to withdraw money for a specific period, ranging from 3 months to 5 years. Early withdrawal could also carry a penalty.

These options do not bring the best returns, but they'll allow you to access your money quickly without penalty (or a minor one in the case of a CD).

Chapter Three:

Debt – The Financial Termite

Hopefully you can skip this chapter because you have no debt, but that's not the reality for most of us. Depending on the pundit or expert to whom you listen, they may talk about the pros and cons of debt. While not all debt is necessarily "bad" debt, it's always preferable to be debt-free. My goal is to get you there.

Tolerable Debt

Real estate can be an incredible wealth builder, but it does not come without risks. In the 2008 financial crisis, home values plummeted. Plenty of families had their homes foreclosed, displacing many. Houses sat on the market for months (sometimes years) before they sold, and many owners lost money. Although some survived the downturn, they still took years to get back into a positive equity position. Thousands were left underwater, meaning they owed more on the house than it was worth.

Mortgage debt can be considered a tolerable debt under the right circumstances. Aim to not buy more house than you can afford and have a high enough credit score to get a good interest rate. You need a home and one day you will hopefully sell that house for much more than you paid for it.

Generally, I recommend that your housing expenses (mortgage, property taxes, homeowner's insurance) account for no more than 30% of your income. You should also aim for a down payment of at least 20% to avoid PMI. Private mortgage insurance is a premium you pay if your down payment is less than 20% of the cost of your home. This insurance does not protect you, but protects the lender in the event you default.

Personally, I do not view primary homes as an investment. A home is a place where you choose to live and raise your family. A home provides safety from the elements and shelter to gather for family holidays. A home is where you and your family make memories. In my opinion, you cannot put a price on the memories and experiences you share with your family and friends.

With that said, let me provide an example of how a home can be a wealth building strategy. Assume you buy a home for $250,000 using a 30-year fixed-rate mortgage at 4%. You put down 20% or $50,000 as a down payment.

Your monthly payment would be $954, excluding homeowner's insurance and property taxes (those will vary on where you live). Total interest paid on the 30-year loan would be $143,739 and your total cost would be $393,739.

Now, let's assume the home appreciates in value at 2% each year. After thirty years, your home would be worth $452,840. This is more than $200,000 higher than what you paid for it. Now to be fair, inflation does factor into this; however, if inflation stays below 2% each year, you have gained. If you sold the home after 30 years, appreciation would recoup your interest expense and give you a $59,000 profit above your total cost. It gets better; when you sell an asset at a profit, it is usually taxed at short-term or long-term capital gains. Holding an asset for longer than twelve months will qualify it for long-term capital gains treatment. This is generally more favorable than the short-term capital gains tax. If you sell the home you've lived in for the last two out of five years, then the profit is tax-free up to $250,000 if you file single or $500,000 if you file jointly.

Bad Debt

Debt is like a financial termite eating away at your peace of mind, cash flow, and ability to invest in your future.

The idea that some bad debts may be good debts has been drummed into our minds; the main culprit being student loans. Think about that for a second. Social norms tell us that getting a college degree (often financed by loans) is the only way to get ahead. Student loans are not inherently bad. Many times, they can provide you with a great education and a degree. A degree that gives a foundation for a career makes the loan worthwhile. Yet, I often see the opposite. Many do not understand how student loans work, they receive a degree they don't and can't use, can't find a job, or find that they don't enjoy the field. They have now become a slave to the debt. A debt acquired that anchors them to the ground and keeps them from reaching their full potential.

For example, if one received a law degree and then decided they didn't want to practice law; this can be crushing debt. It would be tough to pay back six figures of law school debt when you're making $30,000 a year working in retail.

As of 2019, student loans outstanding amounted to over $1,500,000,000,000[2]. Yes, that is one trillion, five hundred billion dollars. This is $420 billion dollars more than all the outstanding credit card debt which is around $1,008,000,000,000[3]. Many individuals have banked on PSLF (Public Service Loan Forgiveness) to have their student loans forgiven. "The PSLF program, established by statute in 2007, forgives borrowers' federal student loans after they make at least 10 years of qualifying payments while working for certain public service employers and meeting other requirements."[4]

The United States Accountability Office conducted a study of student loan borrowers in September of 2018. They found that 1,173,420 borrowers requested to certify their employment in hopes of having their loan forgiven. Of those, only 890,516 borrowers were eligible. Furthermore, there were 19,321

---

[2] https://www.forbes.com/sites/zackfriedman/2019/02/25/student-loan-debt-statistics-2019/#365c081f133f

[3] https://www.federalreserve.gov/releases/g19/current/default.htm

[4] https://www.gao.gov/assets/700/694304.pdf

borrowers who submitted a loan forgiveness application, but only 55 were approved. Even worse, that is 0.0047 percent of all borrowers.[5] This shocked plenty of people. Many see the PSLF program as a way to get a degree and give back to the community. After ten years of service, they hope to have their loans dissolved. In theory this sounds wonderful, but in reality, almost no loans are being forgiven.

Because I love numbers, let's take this one step further. Assume you took out a $25,000 loan at five percent and paid the required 120 monthly payments to qualify for forgiveness. After the 10 years of payments, you would have paid a total of $31,819.33 ($25,000 in principal and $6,819.33 in interest). This is a simplistic example and does not count deferment. How much was actually forgiven? You paid back the principal plus several thousand in interest. Some of the interest was forgiven, but the loan's principal was technically paid back.

While student loan debt can be tolerable, some kinds of debt are undoubtedly bad. For most people, the problem is credit card debt. Credit card debt is easy to get into but hard to get out of. If you pay your card's balance in full each month, the interest rate doesn't matter because you don't pay any interest. Yet, if you carry balances month-to-month, things can get problematic. The interest rate, in the mid-teens to mid-twenties for most cards, is crippling.

One could argue that there are good uses of credit cards such as putting living expenses on a card while between jobs. Ideally you

---

[5] *https://www.gao.gov/assets/700/694304.pdf*

shouldn't do this, and your emergency fund would kick in to help cover these expenses. Plenty of bad uses exist such as buying what you don't need and cannot afford. In the end, it doesn't really matter – you're still in debt.

This isn't to say credit cards are inherently evil. They aren't. Responsible use of a credit card can provide plenty of benefits such as cash back, travel rewards, and consumer protections; however, misusing credit cards is probably the #1 reason people struggle with debt.

If you have unhealthy debt, let's look at ways to get rid of it.

The Snowball and Avalanche Methods of Debt Repayment

Let's explore two effective methods of debt repayment, snowball and avalanche. Both have unique benefits and will work if adhered to. However, one method is superior in my opinion. I'll explain each method before revealing which one is best.

Some debts are less of a priority than others, as explained in the section above. If you have low-interest debt (mortgage, auto, school), you may choose to focus on investing rather than quickly paying these loans. I'll cover that in chapter six. The debts used in the example below are for illustrative purposes.

The snowball method works this way. Make a list of all debts (excluding mortgage debt) by dollar amount, lowest to highest. Here is an example:

1. Student loan #1: $800

2. Visa credit card: $1,200

3. American Express credit card: $2,000

4. Student loan #2: $14,000

Here's how the snowball method would work: focus on paying student loan #1. Pay the minimum and every extra dollar you have in your budget on the debt with the smallest balance. In the meantime, pay the minimum payment on all the other debts. Once you have Student Loan #1 paid off, move on to the Visa credit card. Pay the minimum and every extra dollar you have in your budget, which now includes the amount you were paying on student loan #1. Continue paying only the minimums on all other debts.

Continue doing the same until all the debts are paid off.

The avalanche method works the same way, with one important exception. Rather paying debts in order of lowest to highest dollar amount, list them according to interest rate (highest to lowest).

Using this method, you focus on paying the debt with the highest interest rate first while paying the minimums on the others. Once each debt is paid, add the money you were paying on it towards the next debt on the list.

Both methods have pros and cons. They both work for the same reason. When you focus on paying off just one debt at a time, you can pay them off quicker. Using a "scattergun" method by paying off bits and pieces of your debts is an unorganized approach.

The best part about the snowball method is the feeling that you're making progress on killing your debt. Because you're paying the smaller debts first you can get rid of at least one, if not a few, quickly. It's extremely satisfying to cross a debt off the list, even if it was only a few hundred dollars. The feeling of accomplishment can provide the psychological boost needed to deal with the larger debts.

If you look at both methods strictly from a mathematical standpoint, the avalanche method is superior. When you pay off the highest interest debts first, you pay less interest over time. Interest is what makes it so difficult to get out of debt. But if your high-interest debts have a high-dollar amount, getting them paid off can feel like you're slogging through a quagmire. You're paying as much as you can every month and the debts are still there. This can be enough to make some people give up and it's very demotivating.

In my opinion, snowball method of debt repayment is the best, keeping you focused on paying off your credit card debt, because you see the success faster than you would using the debt avalanche method.

The method that works best is the method you believe will work for you. People don't have to stick to one method. If you like the idea of paying less in interest, start with the avalanche method. If you find yourself getting discouraged with the avalanche method, switch over to the snowball method for a while. Wipe out a smaller debt to reinvigorate your efforts, then switch back to the avalanche method to save money on interest.

A great resource to track your debt repayment strategy is Undebt.it. This service illustrates many payback methods from which to choose. Being able to watch your debt dwindle on this platform is a great motivator.

Get Extra Help

Depending on how good your credit score is, you may be eligible for other debt repayment methods.

One option is to refinance debt through a personal loan. Money can be borrowed at a lower interest rate than you have on current debts and then used to pay off high-interest debts. You still have debt, but it costs less; however, this does not work if more debt exists than the amount you qualify to borrow.

In the past, you had to walk into a bank to get a personal loan. The process could take weeks and require copious documentation. Today this process is quite different. Online lenders have changed the way people borrow money. In today's world acquiring a personal loan is easier and faster, thanks to the internet.

Whether it's a traditional bank offering online loans or a peer-to-peer lender, you can go online and get a loan offer in less time than it will take you to read this chapter. You can browse dozens of offers without impacting your credit score. Once approved, the money can be deposited into your checking account within a few business days.

If you have a great deal of credit card debt, a personal loan can be exactly what you need. You'll save money on interest, simplify your bill paying, and give your credit score a big boost.

Another way to pay off credit card debt quicker is to apply for a 0% introductory APR credit card and do a transfer balance. The new credit card will have a period (usually from 6 to 24 months) during which you pay no interest on the balance you've transferred from another card.

During that time, your entire payment is going toward paying off the balance because interest is not accruing. This can help you pay off debt from an old card quicker. As long as you pay off the balance before the introductory period ends, this is a great debt repayment tool. Once the introductory period ends, the APR reverts to the card's regular rate which you can find online. If you fail to pay the debt before the intro rate ends, the credit card company can go back to the date the card was opened and charge the higher interest rate.

If you have student loan debt, you may be able to refinance through an online lender that specializes in student loan refinancing. Even a half of a percentage point decrease in your interest rate can save you thousands of dollars over the term of your loan.

As with online personal loans, you can browse rates and terms when shopping for a student loan refinance. One important caveat to consider when refinancing. Federal loans come with a set of options for borrowers having trouble making their payments. These include Pay as You Earn, Revised Pay as You Earn, and the Income-Based Repayment Plan. When you refinance your federal student loans, they become private loans and you lose access to those programs.

Private student loans are not eligible for those programs and generally have a higher interest rate. If you have federal loans, think carefully before refinancing. If you have private loans, refinancing is something to seriously consider. You may be able to get a much lower interest rate than you have currently.

Bankruptcy

At some point, you might find yourself doing everything right, but past mistakes still get in the way. If it comes to that, you may consider bankruptcy the best option.

The following story is not a bankruptcy story, but the path that Tom and Mary were on was headed toward bankruptcy. They took some action that was able to prevent bankruptcy, but their effort came with a lot of sacrifice and sleepless nights.

In 2006, Tom and Mary retired and purchased a motor home to become road warriors and travel the country in retirement. They met with their advisor who told them they would be fine to buy a $200,000 motor home.

Fast forward to 2008 and we have the worst financial crisis since the great depression. They lost significant investment money with that advisor and had expenses and a lifestyle they could no longer support. Their social security benefits barely covered their basic living expenses and the remainder of their investments needed to last the rest of their lives.

By 2012 they owed $108,000 on a motorhome that was valued at less than $44,000 and were no longer making payments, damaging their credit, but they had not yet filed bankruptcy. In 2013 the motor home was re-possessed. Mary and Tom feared what might happen next. Should they try to make payments and exhaust their remaining retirement? Should they declare bankruptcy? We went through the financial planning process and consulted an attorney.

After a lot of thought, Tom and Mary offered a $18,000 lump sum to settle the motorhome delinquency. The bank accepted their offer, and they were able to avoid filing bankruptcy and have been repairing their credit.

Although declaring bankruptcy might be the best choice, actually declaring bankruptcy has serious, long-lasting consequences. It does not erase every kind of debt. Bankruptcy is a legal process during which a person or a couple legally declares that they are unable to repay their debt. Two main types of bankruptcy exist: Chapter 7 and Chapter 13.

Chapter 7 bankruptcy will erase these debts: credit cards, medical bills, and personal loans. In return, the debtor (person filing for bankruptcy) allows the trustee overseeing the case to sell certain assets. Most personal belongings such as clothing and furniture may not be sold under Chapter 7. This provides foreclosure protection and forces the mortgage holder to immediately stop foreclosure proceedings. You may still lose your home, but momentarily you'll have some breathing room. During this time, you might be able to catch up on mortgage payments, making it possible to keep your house.

Any money raised from the sale of assets is used to compensate creditors, ranked by a priority system. Debts that are not forgiven under Chapter 7 include: student loans, past due income taxes, child support, alimony, and monetary judgments owed to victims of drunk driving. The process of Chapter 7 bankruptcy usually takes from three to six months.

Chapter 13 bankruptcy does not forgive your debts but reorganizes them. Debtors must make a monthly payment to the trustee in charge of the filing for a period of 36-60 months. The trustee uses those payments to pay creditors who have filed compensation claims. Debtors are not required to sell any personal possessions and filing Chapter 13 will freeze the home foreclosure process.

Not everyone will qualify to file for Chapter 7. A debtor filing for Chapter 7 must have little or no disposable income. A means test is conducted to compare the debtor's average monthly income from the past six months to the median income of a comparable household in the same state. If the debtor's disposable income is below that median, they will be approved to file for Chapter 7.

While bankruptcy does not discharge student loans under Chapter 13, monthly payments can be reduced. A debtor is given the length of the bankruptcy period (36-60 months) to catch up on overdue student loan, mortgage, car, alimony, and child support payments. If you have any loans that required a cosigner, Chapter 13 relieves the financial obligation from the cosigner. Chapter 13 protects assets that a debtor may have been required to sell under Chapter 7. Rather than paying up front, the debtor may be able to spread out payments to his or her bankruptcy attorney over the period of the case.

Filing bankruptcy is a complicated process requiring a great deal of paperwork and documentation, which means an attorney is needed. Attorneys can be expensive and assorted fees must be paid.

Bankruptcy can be a fresh start, but it will destroy your credit for up to ten years. Credit scores can be repaired over time; however, until your score rebounds, you may have a difficulty renting an apartment, buying a car, or being approved for a credit card (perhaps that's not terrible). A credit score doesn't matter most of the time but when it matters, it matters a lot.

Although a great deal of stigma exists around filing bankruptcy, it can be the second chance a person needs to improve his or her financial situation.

Chapter Four:

Financial Goals

We all have goals and dreams. Hopefully, some of your goals are financially related. Our goals have different time frames and that window will help determine what we do with our money. To achieve anything in life, you need a clear vision. As the saying goes: "If you don't know where you are going, how will you know when you get there?" Not having written goals is the number one reason I see people fail. In this chapter, I am going to show you exactly how I teach my clients how to set and pursue goals with a clear vision.

S.M.A.R.T Goals

Goals need to be documented. The simple act of writing down goals on paper helps us to pursue those goals. But simply writing them down isn't enough. You want to create S.M.A.R.T goals. This allows us to see a large goal broken down into more digestible bites.

- Specific: What do you actually want to achieve?

- Measurable: How will you track it?

- Achievable: How can the goal be accomplished?

- Relevant: Why is this goal important to you?

- Time-Bound: When do you want to achieve the goal?

Let's see a S.M.A.R.T goal example.

Specific: Save $1 million by age 50.

Measurable: You can calculate how much you need to invest each month using an online calculator. If you start at age 25, you will need to invest $1,300 a month. This calculation shows us the smaller picture that will help us work toward the larger goal.

Achievable: How can you find $1,300 a month to invest? Your salary might allow for that, maybe you'll have to cut expenses, or you could get a second job to reach that number.

Relevant: Having $1 million by age 50 will mean you're well on your way to being able to retire in the next decade. For most, finding $1,300 a month to invest will be tough. Knowing the benefits behind it will help keep your goal on track.

Time-Bound: Putting a time frame on reaching a goal allows you to see if you need to adjust along the way.

Creating S.M.A.R.T. goals will help you get a realistic view of your dreams. Achieving your goals won't come without hard work and commitment, but you can reach them if you put your mind to it.

Short-Term Goals

Money you're saving for your wedding does not get treated the same way as money saved for retirement. The money you plan to use in the next two to five years is considered short term money. That money can be used for items such as a wedding, home improvement projects, or vacations.

Short term money should be handled much like your emergency fund. The short time frame does not give this money enough time to stay invested through the fluctuations of the market (explained more in the investing chapter). Because of this, it needs to be somewhere relatively low-risk and liquid.

That can include a high-yield (relatively speaking) online savings account, CD, or money market account.

Medium-Term Goals

Medium-term money is money you'll need in five to ten years. Money needed for a down payment on a home, to have a child, or to start your own business.

You can take a bit more risk with this money, especially if you don't have a strict time frame in which you'll need it. For instance, you'd like to buy a home in six years. But if there was a recession six years from now, you could wait it out before pulling your money out of your investments.

A diversified portfolio, perhaps with a 50% stock and 50% bond allocation may be something to consider.

Long-Term Goals

Long-term money is funding you won't need for at least ten years. For most of us, long-term goals mean retirement. It can also signify needs such as paying for a child's college education or buying a rental property.

Retirement money and college money should mainly be invested in tax-advantaged accounts like 401(k)s, IRAs, and 529 plans. This money will not be touched for at least a decade, perhaps several decades. This money will be invested in the higher risk assets, which will hopefully bring higher returns.

Multi-Goal Planning

While short, medium, and long-term goals are important, focusing on the necessity of saving for each separate goal makes prioritizing investments difficult. I prefer to view life as one overarching goal, made up of smaller goals. Once you know what you want to accomplish, you start working your way backward one step at a time. The action of taking these small steps help work toward your larger goals. Creating a multi-goal plan can seem overwhelming, but so is building a house. One doesn't just think to themselves "I am going to build a house" then snap their fingers and have it done. The process takes time and involves many steps such as finding a lot you like, acquiring a loan, hiring a builder, composing building plans, getting building permits, and on and on goes the list.

Starting with a sketched-out plan, which acts as a blueprint for your financial goals, will allow you to make necessary changes as time goes on. Often clients ask me questions:

- "How do I go about planning for multiple goals at one time?"

- "What if my timing changes?"

- "How should I prioritize my goals?"

- A financial vision/action process can help answer these three questions.

Identify Your Core Values: These are three to five core values/fundamental beliefs for you or your family. Examples: A good steward of resources, family is fundamental, philanthropic giving, honesty, integrity, et cetera. Establishing core values will help you create your family's focus.

Establish Your Family Focus: As a family, what is your purpose or passion? This resembles a corporate mission statement and is the overarching goal you want to achieve in life. This statement will encompass many smaller goals along the way. Hopefully, creating one will allow you to look back on your life and accomplishments without regret. An example of a family purpose statement may be living a life free from anxiety about money, providing for the family, or sharing resources with those less fortunate.

Create A 10-Year Target: Imagine where you would like to be ten years from today. The more detailed you can be, the better. This forces you to act towards that specific goal.

A few examples: "I want to retire when I am 55 years old with $1,000,000 in order to travel internationally with my spouse."

"I want to create a charity that supports pediatric cancer patients."

"I will start a business that builds tiny homes for people to live off the grid."

There is no right or wrong ten-year target goal, but it needs to line up with your core values and family focus. This is what drives your passion to pursue your goals.

Chapter Five:

Family and Money

Money can be a taboo topic among families, but it shouldn't be. When a subject is kept in the dark, it can cause strife that carries long-lasting consequences.

Have the Talk

Credit scores and student loan debt aren't appropriate first date conversations. As a relationship becomes more serious (moving in together or getting married), you and your partner need to have "the talk."

This is not an ambush topic. Explain to your partner that since your relationship is changing, you want to put your financial cards on the table and set a date to discuss financial needs and goals. This gives each of you time to gather numbers and prepare yourselves for the discussion. Let the other person know the financial details needed and ask him or her to think about what needs to be known as you begin life together as a couple.

Each couple will have their own list, but these are some basic items for an open discussion:

1. Income

2. Debt, what kind?

3. Savings

4. Investments

5. Credit score

6. Financial goals

7. Thoughts on lending/giving money to family/friends

8. Thoughts on accepting money from family/friends

9. Being a working or stay at home parent

This is not a comprehensive list, but a good starting point for a fact-finding mission. The two of you don't have to agree on all financial needs and goals at this stage, but you do want to understand how each thinks and acts about finances because one of the areas mostly likely to cause arguments and problems in your relationship concerns money and how to use what you earn.

Getting Your Partner on Board

Meeting goals will be difficult (even impossible) if you and your partner aren't on the same page. For example, you want to have a budget and your partner thinks you're being too controlling. Like any situation where you are trying to persuade someone, it's all how you frame it. The two of you are grown adults. No adult likes to be told what to do or to feel as if he or she is being treated like a child.

When you're discussing finances, put it in terms of shared goals. For example: you both want to buy a home in five or so years. That requires a great deal of money. Most people can't make such a large purchase without planning and sacrifice. But buying a home is a shared goal, something the two of you should work toward together.

Not everyone can see goals in abstract ways. If you want to buy a house, work out the numbers together. You need $X for a down payment. You want to buy in five years. Divide $X by 5. That's how much you need to save each year. Now divide $X by 12. That's how much you need to save each month. Sit down together with your budget and see where you can come up with that monthly amount.

Communication is the most important part. Treat each other with respect and listen to your partner's concerns. If you work these factors out early, your relationship will be much more open and honest with less arguments and upheaval.

How to Handle Money in a Relationship

There are three basic ways a couple can handle money:

All In: The two of you commingle all money.

Separate: The two of you keep all money completely separate.

Three Buckets: You each have some separate accounts and some joint accounts.

The sad fact is many marriages will end in divorce. Today this is not quite as dire as they once were. We've all heard the "half of all marriages end in divorce" statistic. In reality, the divorce rate has been falling for the past few decades. A couple who marries today has a 75% chance of staying married[6]. At last, some good news!

Hopefully you don't end up in the 25% minority. If you do end up in the minority, comingling all money can complicate an already unfortunate situation. If abuse existed in the marriage, commingled money is even worse, making it much harder for the abused partner to leave.

Keeping all your money separate could work if the two of you lived separate lives, but that sort of defeats the point of marriage. Having said this, divided finances aren't very realistic or practical.

That leaves us with three buckets. You each keep some money separate, but you also combine some accounts to pay for shared expenses. If you earn your own money, no one has the right to tell you what to do with it. But if you have shared goals, you each

---

[6] *https://www.psychologytoday.com/us/blog/heart-the-matter/201704/do-half-all-marriages-really-end-in-divorce*

must contribute to funding those goals. The three buckets strategy solves this.

Each person can do what they like with their personal bucket of money, no questions asked. The shared bucket goes towards joint expenses and shared goals. Of course, many couples make a disparate amount of money; in which case you cannot put an equal amount into the shared bucket. In that scenario, each person puts in the same percentage, not the same dollar amount.

Children and Money

On average, it costs $233,610 to raise a child to age eighteen.[7] This number excludes college expenses. Having children is one of life's most enjoyable, but expensive decisions. Hopefully, you and your partner discussed whether you wanted children before you married. A couple can compromise on many life choices, but becoming parents is not one of them.

If you do choose to have children, there's much to discuss. Should one parent stay at home and for how long? What kind of education do you want your child or children to have? A single-income family may have to make a lot of sacrifices. The same is true if you prefer to send your child to private rather than public school.

-----

[7] https://www.usatoday.com/story/money/personalfinance/2018/02/26/raising-child-costs-233-610-you-financially-prepared-parent/357243002/

If you choose to have children, teach them about money and personal finance. Remember what I said earlier in the book, many families and schools do not teach personal finance. This is unfortunate. By filling this void, you can give your children an advantage that will last their entire life.

If the lessons are age appropriate, teaching children about money can never start too early. The toddler stage is probably not the right time to explain differences between a Roth and traditional IRA. Yet you can teach them responsibility and accountability through chores. Make sure they understand that money is earned through hard work. If you are blessed with many resources, let them know that their relatives had to make sacrifices for it.

As children earn money, I recommend teaching them the "Big 3" of money: save, spend, and give. Like the 50/30/20 budget we talked about earlier, this is Budgeting for Kids 101. Save 50 percent, spend 30 percent, and give 20 percent.

Saving teaches discipline and patience. We can't have everything we want immediately. When we save up, our money grows, and we can eventually afford what we want. Allowing children some freedom in spending their money is important. You may believe they should save every penny for college; however, to a child, college is a vague and far away stage. They need a bit of instant gratification to reward hard work and discipline. Most importantly, this teaches gratitude for the blessings they have and how to share with others who may be in need.

When your child is old enough (generally thirteen) or starts earning money, you can open a bank account for them. As a parent, you will be the co-owner of this account. Through this, you can teach them about interest rates, fees, and overdrafts.

Once they are earning money, use a simple online tool like Mint to teach your child how to create a budget. Consider opening a custodial investment account with them. You can teach them how to choose investments, how to track performance, and the importance of long-term (buy and hold) investing.

Credit cards are a touchy issue, because they are often the means by which young people dig themselves into a pit of debt. You must be at least eighteen to get a credit card. Although harder to get approved at that age than it was in the past, it's still possible. If your child's first experience with a credit card happens when they're out of the house, there isn't much a parent can do to control spending. You can only hope they remember the lessons they were taught at home.

A parent can also add their child to one of their credit cards before age 18. I believe this is the best way to teach children the importance of using credit cards properly. Parents can see every charge a child makes and can stop a spending problem early.

Some parents give their child a credit card and blindly pay the balance. This action fails to teach them the benefits and consequences. Each year I hire interns to help around the office. One intern's family taught her the right way. Her parents paid the credit card bill while she was in college; however, it came with a limit. She was given a budget/limit every month. She was expected to provide a monthly expense report including tuition, books, food, rent, gas, et cetera. If she did not provide the expense report, they would take away the card, and she had to pay for the above expenses. She was responsible for her own "fun" money, which is why she was working with us, to earn spending money.

Keeping your family in the dark on the subject of money is not wise. Although understandable to protect children from financial worries, hiding problems solves nothing. Just remember, children are more perceptive than we realize. No matter how well you think you're hiding a source of stress in the family, children can pick up on the stress and its causes. If you don't discuss it, a child's imagination makes up all kinds of scenarios (mom and dad are getting a divorce, someone has a serious illness, or someone might lose their job).

This isn't unique to children. Adults also imagine the worst when they don't know what's happening. You don't want to burden your children. You don't have to explain financial problems in detail, but not explaining anything is harmful, causing unnecessary worry for children, and the parent loses a good opportunity to impart important lessons.

Your Parents and Money

There are countless jokes about in-laws, and for good reason. Issues with in-laws can cause a lot of stress in a marriage. Combine this with money problems and you have a double dose of stress.

Your in-laws may offer seemingly well-intentioned gestures, like helping you put a down payment on a home, which can cause problems within a marriage. One spouse may see this as a generous offer, while the other can see it as a means of control or a commentary on your ability to support your family.

The decisions to loan, borrow, or accept money from family members is something a couple should discuss before marriage.

Another issue is parental finances. No one wants to ask their parents how their finances are or if they are in good shape for retirement. A serious illness can throw a wrench in the works. These are topics both partners need to discuss with their parents.

What do you do if your parents are struggling financially? What if their health reaches a point where they can no longer live independently? Do they have enough insurance (or money) to pay for in-home care or a stay in a long-term care facility? Would one partner refuse to put their parents in such a facility, preferring to care for them at home?

If your parents become incapacitated, could you access the necessary documents required to fulfill their wishes? Do they even have those documents in place? What are their wishes?

If you think it's hard to talk about these topics over Sunday dinner, imagine trying to deal with them amid a health crisis.

Unless you are very close to your in-laws, it's probably better for each spouse to discuss these topics alone with their own parents. After the discussion, report back to each other.

Chapter Six:

Investing

Now let's discuss the subject that many people find most intimidating when it comes to personal finance and financial planning. Investing. Don't worry, investing is not as complicated as it is often made out to be. I'm going to explain the basics, which is all anyone needs to know to get started.

Investing Over the Long-Term

When I first joined my father's practice, he told me that investors' decisions were driven by two things: the emotion of fear and the character flaw of greed. Many people find taking the emotion out of investing difficult. This is especially true if they don't have a professional to help guide them in their decision making. Many people fear investing and it's not hard to understand why. If you're a casual consumer of financial news, you often hear bad news (Bernie Madoff, the dotcom bubble, the housing bubble, Black Monday). Financial news, like any other type of news, isn't all negative. Bad news sells and garners the big headlines.

Try to avoid the doom and gloom. Financial news outlets cause hysteria and FOMO (fear of missing out). This can cause people to greedily chase investment returns. Just because it's the hot fad of the moment doesn't mean it is a good long-term decision. Abandoning an investment strategy just because a "talking head" told you to do so is almost always a terrible idea. I call this investing infidelity. You should create a sound investment strategy that you understand and can stick with in the long run.

If you only pay attention to the bad news, it's no wonder you prefer to keep your money laying in a savings account, where you believe it's safe. Many people do not realize that your money isn't truly safe in a savings account. In a way, your money is safe because it is FDIC insured. If the bank goes under, the government will give you back the lost money (up to $250,000 per depositor, per insured bank, for each account ownership category). However, when your money is in a low-yield savings account, it is losing buying power due to inflation. The value of a dollar is determined by what it can buy with its purchasing power. Inflation decreases the purchasing power of dollars.

From 2010 through 2018, the average rate of inflation in the U.S. was 1.8%[8]. We'll call it 2% for simplicity's sake. If a cup of coffee costs $1 now, next year it will cost $1.02 due to inflation. A dollar in 2019 will buy less in 2020. Doesn't sound like much, does it? But over a period of years inflation can be significant. This is especially true for healthcare and higher education costs, which inflate at a rate of 5-6% each year.

---

[8] *https://www.inflationdata.com/inflation/inflation/decadeinflation.asp*

If your money is earning only 1% in a savings account, it's losing 1% of its buying power value each year due to inflation. This means your money isn't as safe as you think.

We not only want to preserve the buying power of our money, but also want to grow these funds. That's why we take the risk of investing. The term "risk" is often misused in the investing world. Let me explain the difference between risk and volatility. Volatility represents the normal price fluctuations in an asset's value. Stocks, bonds, gold, real estate, et cetera fluctuate in value every day. That doesn't necessarily make that investment or asset "risky."

Risk is the probability of permanent loss of value. Now you could invest in assets that are both highly volatile and risky. A risky investment carries a high probability that you will lose your asset. Many investors refer to price fluctuations as risk (rather than volatility); but it is important to understand the difference between the two. How much risk should I take? There is no such thing as a completely risk-free investment. What mitigates the risk of investing is a long-time horizon. As explained in the financial goals chapter, you need to split your money into three buckets: short-term, medium-term, and long-term. Investments placed in the long-term funds are ideal for higher risk.

What the market does in the short-term is not an indicator of its long-term performance. What a stock does in a single year tells nothing about what it will do in the next ten years.

The average annualized total return for the S&P 500 index over the past 89 years, 1928-2016 is 9.8%.[9] That century of data factors in events like the Great Depression and the crash of 2008 that led to the Great Recession.

When you hear the term "stock market," it means the S&P 500. The S&P 500 index is made up of about 500 of America's largest publicly traded companies. It is considered the benchmark measure for annual returns. Measured by the S&P 500 index, stocks return an average of about 10% a year over time.

Remember, we must factor in inflation; meaning that 10% will actually net closer to 7% or 8% each year. When you compare this to the 1% you're losing each year by leaving your money in a savings account, it looks quite nice.

The Power of Compounding Interest

Do you know a millionaire? If you don't know anyone who owns a yacht or a private jet, you might think the answer is "no." Yet you might know many and not even be aware of it. We call this the "millionaire next door" type. In 2018, there were 11.8 million American households with a net worth of more than $1 million (3% of the population).[10]

---

[9] https://www.cnbc.com/2017/06/18/the-sp-500-has-already-met-its-average-return-for-a-full-year.html

[10] https://spectrem.com/Content_Press/press-release-spectrem-groups-2019-market-insights-report.aspx

Even if someone doesn't have a yacht or a private plane, they might have a million dollars. They might work in your office or attend your church. They aren't a mogul or a trust fund baby, so how are they a millionaire? Simple—they likely invested and put the power of compound interest to work for them. They also live life frugally and budget for unexpected expenses.

Compound interest is the earnings added to the principal amount of a deposit or investment. It's interest on interest. It is reinvested so that interest in the next period is earned on the principal amount, plus the accumulated interest.

I know that is confusing. Let's use a simple example. Say you open a savings account and deposit $100. The account earns 1% interest per year. One year after the initial deposit, you've earned $1. The following year, you are now earning interest on $101—not $100; so you earn $1.01. By the end of the second year, you have $102.01.

I know what you're thinking, earning $2.01 over a two-year period won't exactly to allow you to retire. But when it comes to investing, you will hopefully have more time, more money, and higher returns.

I plugged some bigger numbers into a compound interest calculator. You can do the same, as there are plenty of them online.

- $1,000 initial investment

- 30 years invested

- 7% rate of return

- $ 500 per month additional contribution

- Compounded annually

At the end of thirty years, we have invested $181,000 of our own money. Our return is $595,645; which means compound interest made us $414,645. We didn't have to work two jobs to earn this return. We just had to invest, steadily contribute, and leave the money in the market for thirty years. This is likely how the woman in the cubicle next to yours is a millionaire. That is the magic of compound interest.

Let's take it another step further. When you employ a Legacy Planning Strategy, the power of compounding can help you create generation-spanning wealth.

- $10,000 initial investment

- 100 years invested (two or three gen generations from now)

- 10% rate of return (assume we are going to be aggressive since this is long-term)

- No additional money added

- Compounded annually

At the end of that hundred-year period, the $10,000 investment would be worth $137,806,123. Talk about creating a family legacy. A simple $10,000 investment could make your family worth more than $100 million dollars. Even though you won't be around to enjoy the money, those who succeed you will. To quote a Greek proverb: "A society (or family's wealth in our case) grows great when old people plant trees whose shade they know they shall never sit in."

These are hypothetical examples and are not representative of any specific situation. Your results will vary. The hypothetical rates of return used do not reflect the deduction of fees and charges inherent to investing.

Just the Basics

Hopefully, all those large numbers have whetted your appetite, and I've convinced you to start investing. You'll be on your way if you can understand a few basic concepts.

Time Horizon

I explained time horizons in the "Financial Goals" chapter. The sooner you need a bucket of money, the less risk you can afford to take with it. The money that you can use to go "all in" and put into the stock market is your long-term money. You should not need this money for at least ten years.

Risk Tolerance

Risk tolerance is how much market risk (fluctuations in the market and potential losses) you can tolerate. There are calculators online that can help you determine your risk. These tools will ask certain questions such as age, upcoming major expenses, and the time horizon of your investment. It aims to gauge how you would react to an "x" amount of loss in your investment's value.

Based on your answers, you will be categorized as an aggressive, moderate, or conservative investor. These calculators can guide you between being too aggressive (willing to take a great deal of risk) and too conservative (not willing to take much risk at all).

If you are too aggressive, you can lose a lot of money. If you are too conservative, you won't make enough. The two biggest factors in risk tolerance should be age and time horizon. Generally, the younger you are, the more aggressive you can be. The older (closer to retirement) you are, the more conservative you need to be.

Asset Allocation

When we're talking about risk tolerance, this means how heavily your portfolio is weighted between stocks and bonds. Stocks are a riskier investment than bonds, but over time they provide the opportunity for higher returns. The more aggressive you are, the higher percentage of stocks your portfolio will contain.

There is a rule of thumb to determine your asset allocation. Use this simple formula: percentage of stocks= (100 – your age).

- 20 years old: 80% stocks – 20% bonds

- 30 years old: 70% stocks – 30% bonds

While this can be a good place to start, it is a bit too conservative for my taste. I believe that anyone under thirty can go all in. You can set your allocation to 100% stocks and start reducing that by 10% each decade:

- 29 years and under: 100% stocks – 0% bonds

- 30 years old: 90% stocks – 10% bonds

- 40 years old: 80% stocks – 20% Bonds

People are living longer than ever. In fact, studies show that people born in the 2000's (in a developed country) are likely to live to be 100 years old.[11] Our money must outlive us, which is why I recommend the more aggressive allocation. Asset allocation does not ensure a profit or protect against a loss.

Diversification

Diversification is a term you hear often when it comes to investing. This simply means not putting all your eggs into one basket. Say your only investment is in Apple, which is in the technology sector. If this company takes a big plunge, all your eggs get smashed.

You can research plenty of companies across many sectors, but this takes a great deal of time and knowledge that beginning

---

[11] https://www.reuters.com/article/us-ageing-populations/half-of-babies-born-in-rich-world-will-live-to-100-idUSTRE5907DM20091002

investors don't have. The simple way to diversify your investment portfolio is to invest in an index fund.

An index fund is a type of mutual fund or ETF (exchange-traded fund). An investment in Exchange Traded Funds (ETF), structured as a mutual fund or unit investment trust, involves the risk of losing money and should be considered as part of an overall program, not a complete investment program. An investment in ETFs involves additional risks such as not diversified, price volatility, competitive industry pressure, international political and economic developments, possible trading halts, and index tracking errors. The investments inside that fund seek to match or track a specific market index. This could be the S&P 500, NASDAQ, et cetera. These typically carry low operating expenses.

Index funds don't try to beat the market or earn higher returns compared to market averages. Instead, an index fund attempts to "be" the market by holding stock in each firm listed on a particular index. It aims to mirror the performance of that index.

For example, if an index tracks the S&P 500, it buys shares from each company in the S&P 500. As an investor, you buy shares of the index fund in which the value will mirror the gains and losses of the S&P 500.

An index fund allows you to own a basket of stocks across many sectors (tech, pharmaceuticals, industrials, energy, et cetra). Having many eggs in lots of baskets insulates you from risk. Is technology down? That's okay, energy is up.

There is no guarantee that a diversified portfolio will enhance overall returns or outperform a non-diversified portfolio. Diversification does not protect against market risk.

How Much to Invest

In the "Budgeting" chapter, I suggested that you should invest 20% of your net income. That encompasses all your investments. If you're contributing 5% to a 401(k), you have another 15% to invest elsewhere.

I understand that asking you to invest 20% of your income is a tall order. You can work up to it gradually, but you don't want to wait too long. You've seen the beauty of compound interest, but it requires time to work. The longer you wait, the harder it is to make up for lost time.

Be Aware of Fees

Excessive fees can cost you a large amount of your retirement savings. Ask your advisor to disclose their fees and read the prospectus to learn what you're paying on your investments. A prospectus is a detailed document that gives information about a security. It is reviewed by the Securities and Exchange Commission. These can be helpful to read.

There are generally seven types of investment fees:

Expense Ratio: It costs money to run a mutual fund. These costs are paid through a fee called the expense ratio. If a fund has an expense ratio of 0.80%, it means for every $1,000 invested, $8 each year goes toward operating expenses. The expense ratio is deducted from your returns. This fee is buried inside the daily valuation of your investment and is not transparent.

Investment Management Fees: Investment management fees are charged as a percentage of total assets under management. An investment advisor charging 1% means that for every $10,000 you invest, you'll pay $100. This fee is typically deducted from your account quarterly, meaning in this example you would pay $25 per quarter.

Transaction Fees: If you buy individual stocks or mutual funds through a brokerage account, you'll pay a transaction fee each time you buy or sell. The fees typically range from $4.95 to $19.95 per trade.

Front-End Load: Also known as a commission, this fee is charged by mutual funds. If a fund has a front-end load of 5% and you buy shares at $10 each, your shares are worth $9.50 the following day. This is because $0.50 was charged as the front-end load.

Back-End Load: Mutual funds charge a back-end load, or surrender charge, when you sell the fund. The fee usually gets lower as you own the fund longer. For example, a fund may charge a 5% back-end load if you sell within one year then a 4% fee if sold in the second year.

Annual Fee: Brokerage accounts and mutual funds may charge an annual fee or custodian fee, which can range from $25 to $90 per year. Some retirement accounts charge this fee to cover the cost of the required IRS reporting. The fee for these accounts is typically $10 to $50 per year.

Closing Fee: Some firms charge a fee when you close your account, ranging from $25 to $150 or more per account.

Types of Investments

When we hear the word "investing" we often think of stocks, but there are many other types. This isn't a comprehensive list but covers what the average investor should know.

Stocks: When you buy a stock, you have bought a tiny share of ownership in a company. Companies issue stock to raise capital or pay back debt. The price of a stock depends on many factors. External market factors could include a recession, change in monetary policy, sector downturns, or wars. Internal elements that could change a stock price include revenue, profit, earnings, or growth. Stocks are traded on exchanges in which buyers and sellers agree on a price. This is called a secondary market.

Bonds: When you buy bonds, you're essentially loaning money to a company or government body. Your loan is repaid in a predetermined number of years. Before that time, you're paid interest on the bond. Bonds are traded on a secondary market, but it usually is not through an exchange. These markets are decentralized and less formal in how trades are executed. Bonds are subject to market and interest rate risk if sold prior to maturity. Bond values will decline as interest rates rise and bonds are subject to availability and change in price.

Mutual Funds: A mutual fund is composed of a variety of equities under the management of a fund manager. The manager chooses the investments to mitigate unsystematic risk. Mutual funds are one way to diversify your portfolio. They trade at the end of the day. When you buy or sell a mutual fund, you are transacting at the price on the close of a particular trading day.

Exchange-Traded Funds: An ETF is an fund containing a variety of investments. These may include stocks, bonds, or commodities. An ETF provides diversification and often has low fees. They have become quite popular in the last decade. ETFs trade throughout the trading day. When you buy or sell one, you are transacting in real time.

Real Estate/REIT: A REIT is a real estate investment trust. The fund holds individual properties instead of stocks and bonds. Investors buy shares in a REIT to receive rental income and benefit from a property's appreciation. Typically, you want to stay away from REITs as interest rates rise. Investing in Real Estate Investment Trusts (REITs) involves special risks such as potential illiquidity and may not be suitable for all investors. There is no assurance that the investment objectives of this program will be attained.

Types of Accounts

401(k): Many are introduced to investing through this method, as some employers offer them as a way to save for retirement. A 401(k) usually contains mutual funds and provides tax advantages. For 2019, the maximum allowable contribution for a 401(k) is $19,000. But if you're over age 50, there is a "catch-up contribution limit" which means you can contribute an additional $6,000.

IRA: There are two basic types of IRAs, traditional and Roth. Both are tax-advantaged retirement accounts. The main difference between the two is when and how you get the tax advantage. When you contribute money to a traditional IRA, it is tax-deductible for the year, up to certain phase outs. This can lower your taxable income. A Roth IRA lets you withdraw money during retirement without being taxed on it. The maximum contribution for IRAs in 2019 is $6,000; and the catch-up contribution limit is an additional $1,000. This chart is helpful in comparing the two:

Traditional IRA	Roth IRA
In most cases, contributions are tax deductible.	Contributions are not tax deductible.
There are no annual income limits on contributions.	In 2019, you can contribute up to the limit if your modified adjusted gross income is less than $137,000 for singles and $203,000 for couples.
You must make annual withdrawals from your IRA after you turn 70 ½.	No withdrawals required if you are the original owner.
You must pay taxes on withdrawals in retirement.	You are not taxed on qualified withdrawals in retirement.

Limitations and restrictions may apply. Future tax laws can change at any time and may impact the benefits of Roth IRAs. Their Tax treatment may change.

Building a Portfolio

A sensible introduction to investing is through your employer-sponsored 410(k). It's easy, automated, and you can accrue free money if your employer offers matching. If you like the 401(k) options offered and they carry reasonable fees; max out this account. The most important thing to invest in is retirement. Doing so with a tax-advantaged account like a 401(k) is wise. If your plan has poor options, contribute the least amount needed to qualify for matching; but you may not want to max out your contribution.

Once your 401(k) is in order, focus on setting up an IRA. I recommend this for same reason as a 401(k): tax advantages.

The options above have penalties for early withdrawal. Because retirement accounts lock up your money for many years, you want to invest in a non-retirement asset. Consider ETFs (exchange-traded funds) because of their diversification and low fees. This type of investment should not be used as a bank account, but the money does not have to be invested for several decades (although it can be).

You may want to consider adding a bit of real estate to your portfolio. Should you include your home as part of your real estate portfolio? I don't believe so, though many will disagree. An investment is something that seeks to makes money. We have been convinced by agents and mortgage brokers that our home should hold the majority of our equity. In most cases, your primary residence ends up costing money even after the mortgage is paid off. One still must pay for items such as property taxes, HOA fees, repairs, and maintenance. You might make money when you sell your home, but that isn't guaranteed. When it comes to adding real estate to your portfolio, I prefer rental properties or REITs. To start, consider allocating somewhere between 5% and 10% of your portfolio to this sector. It is important to note that investing in Real Estate Investment Trusts (REITs) involves special risks such as potential illiquidity, in other words being hard to convert to cash, and may not be suitable for all investors. There is no assurance that the investment objectives of this program will be attained.

I've explained why I'm not a big proponent of hoarding cash, but I do feel that a fully funded emergency fund is an important part of your portfolio. Your rainy-day fund can help prevent you from dipping into the investments in your portfolio.

What about buying individual stocks? I do not recommend it for beginning investors. Investing in single stocks requires a fair bit of research to make an informed decision. If that interests you, that's okay, but it usually does not appeal to the average person. Even if you do carry out enough research, this is not where you put your rent money. If you are going to buy individual stocks, only use money you can "afford" to lose.

There you have it, a potential portfolio in a just a few paragraphs!

Is it Ever too Late to Start Investing?

The best time to plan a tree is twenty years ago. The second best time is today. The same applies to investing. It's never too late to start investing and there is no age limit. Yet investing enough for retirement can be tough if you wait too long. Therefore, you should not delay the matter any longer.

Hypothetically, let's say you started $200 each month in an ETF when you were 25 years old. With an average yearly return of 6%, you would have about $32,800 after ten years. If you didn't make any further contributions or touch the money until age 65, you'd have almost $200,000.

Now let's imagine you wait until you are 45 to start investing. Let's say you contribute $250 per month. With the same 6% return and leaving the money untouched until age 65, you'd only end up with about $115,500. Compare this to the 25-year-old example and you can understand the difference. This is the power of compounding interest and time. This is a hypothetical example and is not representative of any specific situation. Your results will vary. The hypothetical rates of return used do not reflect deduction of fees and charges inherent to investing.

The longer you wait to invest, the shorter your time horizon is. This means you cannot take as much risk with your money. If you've sat on the sidelines for too long, the best way to proceed is to max out your retirement accounts.

Chapter Seven:

Retirement Investing

The money saved for retirement is the most important money of your entire financial plan. You may choose not to buy a home or to make children pay for college, but you need to have enough money to live on when you no longer work.

Planning to live on Social Security during retirement? Think again. According to the Social Security Administration, the estimated average monthly payment in 2019 was only $1,461[12], which equates to $17,532 a year. To live on this amount would be difficult. Many people expect to spend less during retirement, but rising medical costs often hinder this wish. Assuming Social Security will still be solvent in the future is a mistake. Will it be there? Probably. Can you count on it? Absolutely not.

From a young age my father told me: "If there is activity, there will be money. If there is no activity, there will be no money. You

---

[12] https://www.ssa.gov/news/press/factsheets/colafacts2019.pdf

can only control your own activities. Do not make assumptions or put your fate in someone else's control." This applies to retirement savings as well.

Retirement seems distant for many individuals. People should be preparing to live longer due to healthcare and technology advancements. Taking steps to build a nest egg can help you maintain your lifestyle throughout your retirement years.

In this chapter, we will discuss types of retirement accounts, how to track progress, back-door Roth conversions, and rollover strategies.

Common Retirement Accounts

Although many types of retirement accounts exist, we will only discuss the commonly used ones. When spreading your money across various investments, retirement should always come first. Tax advantages explain this reasoning. I'll cover the basic retirement accounts and explain the tax benefits of each.

401k

We previously touched on the basics of this option, but let's go deeper. This is a pain-free way to invest, as your contribution is automatically deducted from each paycheck. Because it is pre-allocated, you are less likely to waste these earnings. If your employer offers matching, you should take advantage of the extra money offered by your employer. Even if you have credit card debt or other obligations, you should contribute the minimum amount to receive matching funds.

Like an IRA, a 401(k) can be built in a traditional or Roth form. Not every company offers both options. You should look at your summary plan description (more on that later) for more information regarding the details. Traditional 401(k) contributions are considered pre-tax dollars, meaning you don't pay taxes on it until you withdraw the money. This means that your taxable income is lowered, potentially saving money for that year.

When you start to withdraw 401(k) money during retirement, you will finally pay taxes on it. Most retired people have a lower income during retirement, which means they are in a lower tax bracket than when they were working. This means your tax burden will likely be reduced.

You cannot withdraw money from your 401(k) until you reach age $59^{1/2}$. If you take money out before that age, you may have to pay income tax on the withdrawn amount and pay a 10% penalty. As with all rules, there are exceptions. Some withdraws may still be taxed as ordinary withdrawals but won't be charged the 10% penalty. These are the main exceptions:

1. In the event of your death, the money in the account will be distributed to named beneficiary or beneficiaries.

2. You roll over one 401(k) into another (or into an IRA). This is common when changing jobs. Rollovers keep their tax-deferred status, allowing the money to be moved without penalty if it is moved to another IRA.

3. You over-contributed and are making a withdrawal to correct the overage.

4. You become permanently disabled.

5. You are age 55 or older and retired early.

6. You use the withdrawal for medical expenses that have exceeded 10% of your adjusted gross income.

Because these withdraws can be considered taxable income, they could push you into a higher tax bracket. You'll also lose the gains that money could have made if it remained invested. If you have an emergency fund, the money in that fund should take care of any reason for withdrawing funds from your 401(k).

A Roth 401(K) works a bit differently. These contributions are not tax deductible at the time contributed. Yet the contributions and the money they earn grow tax-free. There is no tax on Roth IRA withdrawals during retirement (after age 59 ½). Roths have another perk that traditional IRAs don't. You can withdraw the money you have added (but not the earnings on those contributions) without penalty at any time.

A 401(k) usually has mutual funds within it. Most employers offer a variety of choices, each with a different level of risk. Many of the choices will include a target-date fund, which has a calendar year in the name (2040 Target Date Fund). A target-date fund is a good choice for those who prefer a hands-off approach to investing. The asset allocation in these funds automatically becomes more conservative as the target date approaches. The target date is the approximate date when investors plan to start withdrawing their money. The principal value of the fund is not guaranteed at any time, including at the target date.

Other choices may offer model portfolios. This is a selection of investments tailored to you based on surveys. These questionnaires will ask about preferences such as risk tolerance and time horizon.

Traditional IRA

A traditional IRA is a tax-advantaged Individual Retirement Account. Within an IRA, you can buy investments such as mutual funds, individual stocks, and bonds. The contributions are tax-deductible, and you don't pay taxes on them until you withdraw the money during retirement.

If you want to choose your own investments, you can open an IRA through an online brokerage account. If you prefer to let someone else do the choosing, you can open an IRA through a CERTIFIED FINANCIAL PLANNER™ Professional. They will guide you through the investment process.

Like a traditional 401(k), you can't withdraw money from your traditional IRA until you reach age 59 ½. If you take money out before that age, you may have to pay income tax on the withdrawn amount and pay a 10% penalty. Some exceptions to this rule exist. Some withdraws may still be taxed as ordinary income but won't be charged the 10% penalty. These are the main exceptions, as of November 2019:

1. In the event of your death, your beneficiary can withdraw the money penalty-free; but will pay income tax on each distribution.

2. You use the withdrawal for medical expenses that have exceeded 10% of your adjusted gross income.

3. If you lose your job and collect unemployment for 12 consecutive weeks, you can withdraw money without penalty. This money must be used to pay for health insurance for yourself, spouse, or dependents.

4. IRA distributions can be taken to pay for educational expenses. This money is considered taxable income and could impact financial aid eligibility.

5. You can withdraw up to $10,000 ($20,000 for a couple) from an IRA to buy or build a first home without penalty.

6. Those with severe physical/mental disabilities can withdraw without penalty if their doctor says they can no longer work.

7. Military reservists can take IRA distributions without penalty during active duty lasting more than 179 days.

Roth IRA

Like a traditional IRA, a Roth IRA is a retirement account that holds your investments, not an investment itself. There is an important difference between the two IRAs when it comes to the way they're taxed. Roth contributions are not tax deductible at the time they are put in but the contributions and the money they earn grow tax-free. There is no tax on Roth IRA withdraws during retirement (after age 59 ½). This is similar to the difference between traditional and Roth 401(k)s.

There are income limitations and phase out amounts to be aware of when considering if an IRA or ROTH IRA is right for you.

Retirement Investing for the Self-Employed

One of the disadvantages of being self-employed is the lack of access to an employer-sponsored 401(k). But if you own your own business, you still have plenty of options for retirement investing. You will feel better when you see the contribution limits for some of these accounts.

IRA: You can start an IRA, traditional or Roth. The contribution limits are the same, $6,000 for 2019, with an additional $1,000 for those aged 50 and older. *Subject to phase outs.*

Solo 401(k): This account is for those business owners with no employees. The limit in 2019 was $56,000, with an additional $6,000 for those ages 50 and older or 100% of earned income (whichever is less). This account works the same way an employer-sponsored 401(k) works. The contributions are made pre-tax and withdraws after age 59½ are taxed. You can open a solo 401(k) through a brokerage account.

SEP IRA: This account is for those business owners with no employees or with a small number of employees. The contribution limit for 2019 was $56,000 or up to 25% of compensation/net earnings (whichever is less). There is a $280,000 limit on compensation that can be used to factor that contribution. The contribution is tax deductible and the distributions are taxed as income in retirement. A SEP IRA can be opened through a brokerage account.

SIMPLE IRA: This account is for large businesses with a hundred employees or fewer. The contribution limit is $13,000 for 2019 and an additional $3,000 for those aged 50 and older. The contributions are deductible and withdraws during retirement are taxed as income. You can open a SIMPLE IRA through a brokerage account.

Now that we have talked about the types of accounts, I want to discuss retirement investing topics in more depth.

401(k)

One of the most important documents in the 401(k) plan is the summary plan description (SPD). This required document is designed to explain (in understandable terms) how the plan operates and what it will provide. Some of the questions that summary plan descriptions will answer are[13]:

1. Name and type of plan

2. Plan's requirements regarding eligibility

3. Description of benefits and when participants are entitled to those benefits

---

[13] *https://www.irs.gov/retirement-plans/plan-participant-employee/401k-resource-guide-plan-participants-summary-plan-description*

4. Statement that the plan is maintained, pursuant to a collective bargaining agreement (if applicable

5. Statement about whether the plan is covered by termination insurance from the Pension Benefit Guaranty Corporation

6. Source of contributions to the plan and the methods used to calculate the amount of contributions

7. Provisions governing termination of the plan

8. Procedures regarding claims for benefits and remedies for disputing denied claims

9. Statement of rights available to plan participants under ERISA

A few years ago, I was working with a client who made over $100,000 a year. She was a busy commercial banker for a local bank. In fact, she was employee number seven for that bank. Between her salary and bonus, she had maxed out her 401(k) contributions by May.

This is called front-loading your 401(k). She was receiving the full match from her employer. Shortly before I started working with her, the bank was acquired by a regional bank. She kept making her contributions after the acquisition. Upon reviewing her SPD, we found that she was missing out on a significant amount of match from the new company. The summary plan description explained that company matches were paid per pay period. This meant she had to contribute during all the pay periods to receive the full employer match.

Let's look at an example. Assume a company will match 100% of an employee's contribution up to 6% of their $100,000 salary. In 2019, the maximum employee-deferral amount was $19,000 for those under 50 years old. If there are twenty-four pay periods in a year, an employee would need to contribute $791 each pay period to max out the $19,000 limit. If done, they will receive the full match from the employer, which would be $250 per period or $6000 per year.

If the employee decided to contribute $1,000 per pay period, contribution limits would be maxed out by the 19th pay period. That employee would miss out on $250 in contributions for the remaining 5 pay periods. The total missed matches would be $1,250.[1] [2] This may not sound like much, but over time, the lost growth can mean a significant missed opportunity.

Strategies for 401(k)s

A question I often get is: "I recently changed jobs. What should I do with my old 401(k)?" There are several options to evaluate when changing jobs.

Cash Out Your 401(k): Many people choose to cash out their 401(k) plan when they leave their employer. It is easy to see why this is tempting. Often people view their 401(k) balance as a "bonus" and use it to pay bills, buy something special, or boost their savings account.

Despite the temptation, cashing out a 401(k) is not a wise decision, especially if you are under the age of 59½. Taxes must be paid on the amount that is withdrawn and there is a 10%

penalty if withdrawing before age 59½. Between the taxes and penalties, a significant portion of the balance is lost. This can be avoided if you move the money into a qualified account.

Leave Funds at Your Former Employer: If the balance is below a certain threshold ($500 for example) the plan's custodian may cut you a check for the remaining amount. However, it is possible to leave money in the plan indefinitely. This depends on what the plan stipulates as the minimum level of money to keep the account open.

If you leave money in the old 401(k), inconveniences might come from dealing with your former employer. Navigating the former employer's 401(k) platform and human resources department may be challenging. It could also create a problem for your beneficiaries. If you pass away, your beneficiaries will need to use a death certificate to file a death benefit claim on your investment accounts. Do they know where your investments are? Are they aware of your old 401(k)? If you switch jobs many times, will they be able to track down your investments across many employers?

Transfer Funds to Your New Employer: You may have the option to rollover funds from a previous employer's 401(k) into your new employer's 401(k) plan. This allows you to consolidate retirement assets into one plan. One plan is easier to track and manage while continuing the tax deferral potential. However, your 401(k) options may be limited when compared to an IRA. You will also be subject to the new administration of the plan including management fees, transaction limits, and investment options.

Roll Funds into an IRA: You have the option to roll the funds out of the 401(k) and into an IRA with no penalty or tax liability. This gives you more control over the investments. Inside of an IRA, you can select a wide variety of financial/insurance products (stocks, bonds, international stocks, and more). Inside of a traditional IRA, your funds grow tax-deferred until you make withdrawals. Withdrawing money after age 59½ allows you to avoid the 10% penalty for early withdrawal. At age 70½, you are required to start making withdrawals.

Roth Strategies

The final strategies I will discuss are the backdoor Roth conversion and the mega backdoor Roth conversion. These are complicated strategies, but it may be worth the trouble. These can supercharge your retirement savings.

Backdoor Roth IRA Conversion: High-income earners have started utilizing a technique called a "backdoor" Roth conversion. This is for high-income earners who are phased out by the IRS rules on IRA or Roth IRA contributions.

Here are the phase-out ranges for 2019, according to the IRS[14]:

1. For single taxpayers covered by a workplace retirement plan, the phase-out range is $64,000 to $74,000 (up from $63,000 to $73,000).

---

[14] https://www.irs.gov/newsroom/401k-contribution-limit-increases-to-19000-for-2019-ira-limit-increases-to-6000

2. For married couples filing jointly, if the spouse making the IRA contribution is covered by a workplace retirement plan, the phase-out range is $103,000 to $123,000.

3. For an IRA contributor who is not covered by a workplace retirement plan but married to someone who is, the deduction is phased out if the couple's income is between $193,000 and $203,000.

4. For a married individual filing a separate return who is covered by a workplace retirement plan, the phase-out range is not subject to an annual cost-of-living adjustment and remains $0 to $10,000.

This is a two-step strategy that allows high-income earners to move their investment contribution into a Roth. These investors are prohibited from making a Roth contribution and cannot receive a tax deduction for making a traditional IRA contribution. The "backdoor" strategy fixes this problem.

For those under 50, the max contribution in 2019 was $6,000. For those older than 50, you can make a $1,000 "catch-up" contribution totaling $7,000. The first step entails making a non-tax-deductible traditional IRA contribution. The second step requires you to convert this IRA to a Roth IRA. You want to be careful of the step-doctrine, although this is a less prevalent issue now that Congress passed the Tax Cuts and Jobs Act Bill. Consulting a CERTIFIED FINANCIAL PLANNER™ Professional or CPA is the best way to ensure proper execution of this strategy.

Mega-Back Door Roth Conversion: The mega backdoor Roth conversion operates like the previous strategy, but it acts inside of a 401(k). This earned the "mega" tag because the contribution limits on 401(k)s are substantially higher. In 2019, the contribution limit for those under 50 years old is $19,000. For those over 50 years old, it is also $19,000; but it adds a $6,000 "catch-up" provision, which allows for a total of $25,000.

If your 401(k) allows after-tax contributions and in-service conversions, you can deposit above your max contribution amount. Follow that step by converting after-tax contributions into a Roth.

For 2019, the maximum allowable amount towards a 401(k) plan is $56,000[15]. If you utilize this strategy, make sure contributions, employer matches, and after-tax contributions do not push you over the $56,000 limit.

The above are all viable options but may not be suitable for everyone. I encourage you to reach out to CERTIFIED FINANCIAL PLANNER™ Professional who can guide you through the investment process and create a plan that works for your goals and objectives.

---

[15] *https://www.irs.gov/retirement-plans/plan-participant-employee/retirement-topics-401k-and-profit-sharing-plan-contribution-limits*

Chapter Eight:

Know Your Numbers

Unsurprisingly, there are plenty of numbers involved in personal finance and financial planning. While not all are relevant to everyone, some numbers you should just know.

Your Credit Score

Your credit score is a number that tells potential lenders (banks, credit card companies, peer-to-peer lenders) how much of a risk you are. They want to measure how likely you are to repay borrowed money, whether it's for a mortgage or for a credit card bill.

Your credit score is determined by the information in your credit report. A credit report tracks the payment history for different types of bills, student loans, personal loans, car loans, mortgages, credit cards, and sometimes rent/utilities.

Your report many include bills sent to collection agencies, repossessed items, home foreclosures, or bankruptcies. The companies that collect this information are known as credit bureaus. The United States has three major ones: Experian, TransUnion, and Equifax. Each bureau may have different information about each consumer, but sometimes this information can be incorrect. I'll discuss how to address potentially incorrect information later in this chapter.

Based on the information on your credit report, you will be given a credit score. There are various credit score models, but FICO is the most widely used. Here are their benchmarks:

Excellent: 800-850
Very Good: 750-799
Good: 700-749
Fair: 650-699
Poor: 600-649
Very Bad: 300-599

Your credit score is made up of five factors:

Payment History 35%: Your payment history includes payment timeliness on loan and credit accounts, accounts you are currently over 30 days behind on, bankruptcies, court-ordered debt payments, overdue accounts sent to collection agencies, how many days past due on delinquent accounts, and the dollar amount of your past due accounts.

Amounts Owed 30%: Factors considered are your utilization ratio (see explanation in next paragraph), the number of accounts on which you carry a balance, and how much you owe on current credit cards/installment loans. This shows potential lenders how sustainable your spending habits are and also explains how likely you are to have serious financial problems in the future.

Utilization is how much available credit you have in comparison to your total credit. Ideally, this number should be 30% or lower. Let's use a simple example. If you have two credit cards, each with a $500 limit, you have a total available credit of $1,000. To have favorable utilization, you should owe no more than $300 across both cards. That would give you a utilization rate of 30%.

Length of Credit History 15%: The amount of time you've been using credit matters. Looking back over many years of data gives the lender a more complete picture. Many that have trouble getting approved for a credit card or a loan don't necessarily have "bad" credit. These people have what is known as a "thin" credit file, meaning they don't have a very long credit history. Lenders do not like this.

For most of us, our student loans are the oldest in our credit files.

New Credit 10%: This is how many lines of credit you've recently opened and how that number compares to the total number in your credit history. It also includes when you opened your most recent account, how many times you've applied for credit (hard-pull) in the last twelve months, and how long ago your last credit inquiry was made.

Potential lenders look at this is an indicator of how desperate a borrower is for credit. Typically, people only apply for multiple lines of credit if they are in dire need of money. A low rating in this area waves a red flag to lenders.

Types of Credit Used 10%: This factor shows the different kinds of credit accounts you have used and how recently you used them. Different types include credit cards, retail lines of credit, student loans, personal loans, car loans, and mortgages.

Generally, the more variety you have, the better.

It's easy to get your credit score today. You can create an account on sites like Credit Karma and Credit Sesame. Many credit cards will include a free credit score, which you can see on your statement or by logging into your online account.

What credit score should you aim for and why does it matter? Do you need an 850? No, if you can get your score up to 760, that's good enough; but good enough for what? To get the best interest rates on loans. And that matters a lot. The lower your interest rate, the cheaper it is to borrow money for things like real estate, cars, starting a business, or refinancing existing loans. If you have a score of 760 or higher, you'll be offered the best interest rates on loans.

For credit cards, it doesn't matter as far as interest rates are concerned. The annual percentage rate (APR) is the same for everyone. The only reason credit matters in this area is that a credit score of 760 or higher means you're more likely to be approved for premium rewards cards. This could bring perks like cash back, free flights, and hotel stays.

Should I worry if my credit score isn't at 760? Only if you're soon looking to borrow money for something like a home or car. If you are thinking of borrowing money in the mid to distant future, your score can be improved. This will ensure that when you are ready to borrow money, you can get the best interest rate.

Improve Your Credit Score

As I explained, it is possible that the information on your report can be wrong. In fact, 26% of those polled in a survey by the FTC found at least one error on their reports. Each year, consumers are entitled to a free copy of their credit report from each of the three major credit bureaus. You can visit the website "Annual Credit Report" to request copies of all three reports. There are plenty of other sites purporting to offer free credit reports and some of these are just paid credit monitoring sites. You can track your own credit by reading over your credit report, so don't use any other source than the one listed here:

https://www.myfico.com/credit-education/credit-reports/fixing-errors

Read through each report and look for the following:

Incorrect Personal Information: Be sure all parts of your name are spelled correctly. If this information is wrong, a different person with a variation of your name may be on your report. Verify that your address, Social Security number, and employment information is correct.

Bad Debts Older than 7 Years: Any bad debt seven years or older should be removed from your report.

Duplicate Accounts: Occasionally an account will be listed twice, which makes it look like you have more open credit and more debt.

Debts from An Ex-Spouse: If you're divorced or getting divorced, remove your name from any accounts you and your spouse held jointly so you won't be held liable for future debts. Check your credit report to make sure no new debts appear from your former spouse.

Correcting Errors on Credit Reports

If you find an error/errors on your credit report, you can dispute them, and credit bureaus are required to investigate within 30-days (unless your dispute is deemed "frivolous").

You can dispute the errors online through each of the three major credit bureaus. You'll need to do the following:

1. List the item or items you're disputing.

2. Explain why this information is erroneous and provide information verifying so.

3. Request the erroneous information be removed from your report.

Keep all correspondence between yourself and the credit bureaus. While they are required to remove incorrect information from your report, you may have to follow up to ensure that it gets done.

You will also need to contact the creditor that provided the incorrect information to the credit bureau. Let them know why you're disputing the information they sent to the credit bureau and provide any proof you have. If a creditor reports the same information to the credit bureau again, it must also include a notice that you're disputing the information.

This process can take thirty to ninety days. Once you have your credit report cleaned up, your credit score may increase. It's a good idea to order a copy of your credit report from each of the three bureaus once per year (which is free). Order from a different one every four months, that way you can track information across all three bureaus. This way, you do not have to pay for a copy of your report but can catch and resolve errors quickly.

Never Miss a Payment

You can see that the biggest factor in your credit score is making payments on time. Whatever you do, never miss a payment. Not only does it hurt your credit score, but they may charge a late fee as well. Set an alert on your phone a day or two before a bill is due and find a time that is convenient for you to sit down and pay it.

Consider setting up auto-payments. I only recommend this if you trust the company to withdraw the correct amount from your account. Even then, always review your payments. Mistakes happen and you don't want $1,500 drafted from your checking account when it was supposed to be $150.

Some companies will allow you to choose the date on which your payments are due, typically credit card companies. Grouping due dates can save you a great deal of time. Just be sure your cash flow can handle paying several bills at a time.

Lower Utilization

If you're in credit card debt your utilization may be high. The obvious fix to this problem is to pay off the debt. I know, that's easier said than done. You can use a personal loan to pay off your debt, but an alternate way exists. This will not be appropriate or possible for everyone, but it does work.

When you are approved for a new credit card there is a small but temporary hit to your credit score. Yet having more available credit lowers utilization and makes up for the ding on your report. Therefore, you could technically open up new cards to help. If you don't use credit cards responsibly, this is not for you. If you cannot handle having extra cards, this will send you even deeper into debt. This is only for those who have learned to control their spending. If your credit score is too low to get approved, by applying you'll still get a hard pull on your report, thus lowering your credit score.

You can get your score from Credit Karma and it will recommend cards you're likely to be approved for based on that score. There's no sense in applying for cards for which you won't be approved.

Handling new credit cards requires a balance. On one hand, you do not want to run up a list of charges you cannot pay. On the other, you do not want to not make any charges, or the issuer will close the account for lack of use. If you find a happy medium, your credit score will reflect on-time payments. Put a recurring monthly charge, like your gym membership on the new card, set it to auto-pay, and hide the card where it won't tempt you. Now you have lowered your utilization and added an on-time payment, both of which will increase your credit score.

What Not to Do

Finally paying off a credit card is extremely satisfying. You might think the next step is to call up the credit card company to cancel the card. This is a bad idea. It seems counter-intuitive, but as you saw, the two things that make up your credit score are utilization and length of credit history. When you cancel a card, you raise your utilization and lower your age of credit history.

Know Your Worth

Your net worth that is! Your personal worth is priceless. Your net worth is the dollar amount found when you sum all your assets and debts. It's quite possible that your net worth will be negative. If you're relatively young and have student loan debt/mortgage debt, having a negative net worth is normal.

What counts as an asset?

1. Cash

2. Investment accounts (including retirement accounts)

3. Real estate (subtracting loans)

4. Automobiles (subtracting loans)

5. Household items that hold resale value

6. Life insurance policies with a cash surrender value

What counts as a liability?

1. Credit card debt

2. Student loan debt

3. Mortgage debt amount outstanding

4. Auto debt amount outstanding

5. Personal loan debt

If you have $80,000 in assets and $100,000 in liabilities, your net worth is -$20,000. It's important to know your net worth because it gives you an overview of your financial health. Of course, the goal is to have a positive net worth number, one with plenty of zeros. Having a positive net worth is the first goal to work towards.

Your Retirement Number

Working toward a goal is difficult when you don't have an end point. That's the trouble with knowing your retirement number, or how much you need to save for retirement. None of us can predict the future, so it can be difficult to pin down a number. Many of us can't plan for the following week, let alone decades from now. Will your mortgage be paid off? Will you be able to work until retirement age? How much higher will the cost of living be in the future? Those are questions no one can answer.

It never hurts to make some predictions. By doing some basic calculations, you will get a ballpark estimate that can allow you to track progress and adjust along the way. This is preferable to waiting until the end and realizing you haven't saved enough.

There is a well-known personal finance technique to learn your retirement number. Each year you need to save enough to live on 75%-85% of your pre-retirement income. Your retirement number should not be based on your income, rather your projected expenses. You may even need less than you think. If you've paid off your mortgage, moved to a place with a lower cost of living, or downsized from two cars, you could be in good shape.

Don't misunderstand; saving too much is always better than saving too little. You want your retirement goal to be realistic and don't want to forego enjoyment of the money you worked hard to earn.

Here's my preferred method of calculating your retirement number. Estimate how much money you want to live on each year and multiply that number by 25. That number is your retirement number goal.

Here's an example. You want to live on $50,000 each year while retired. $50,000 x 25 = $1.25 million is your retirement number goal.

Now that we have that number, how can we get a number for estimated expenses? Your biggest clue is to look at your current yearly spending. Now subtract items you likely won't be spending money on during retirement such as:

1. A mortgage (though even a paid-off house costs money so housing cost will never be $0)

2. Retirement account contributions

3. Commuting costs

4. Children expenses

5. Professional clothes

6. Payroll taxes

Of course, you may have expenses during retirement that you didn't have during your career that you'll need to add to your expenses which might include:

1. Supporting adult children for whatever reason

2. Supporting elderly parents

3. An expensive health condition, not covered or entirely covered by Medicare

What about Social Security? Should you include it in your calculations? I do not believe that Social Security will go away completely, at least not in the lifetime of anyone reading this. But would I bet my retirement money on it? No, and you shouldn't either.

Each year you get a form from Social Security showing the amount you're eligible for based on the amount of your current contributions. Whatever that number is, don't factor it into your retirement budget but look at it as "bonus" money you might receive.

These are all strategies to consider, but you should meet with a CERTIFIED FINANCIAL PLANNER™ Professional to set a customized plan that works for your current financial status and future goals.

Chapter Nine:

Hiring Financial Help

Now that you are well into the book, you might be feeling overwhelmed. You may be considering hiring someone to guide you through this process so you can spend more time doing what you love. This is understandable, as money carries anxiety, and many people need a coach to help them along the way.

I'll explain when/why you should hire a financial advisor and how to find one who will look after your best interests. The number one reason most people don't hire a financial advisor is because of fees. Yes, it does cost money to have a professional give you advice and guidance on your finances. Many talking heads in the personal finance world will tell you that you can take a "DIY" approach to your financial future. For some people this is true, but it certainly isn't for everyone. Putting yourself into the wrong camp can be a costly mistake.

Hiring a financial advisor is not so different from hiring a trainer or a dietitian. It's not like you don't know how to exercise or what foods are healthy to eat. But those areas are not in your area of expertise. Hiring a professional can help you get the most out of your work out, meal plan, and money.

You don't hire a professional to tell you what you already know. You hire a professional to be an accountability partner. It's easy for me to hit the snooze button in the morning and skip my workout. If I'm paying a trainer, I know I'll receive a call and a hard time for skipping a workout. This forces me to get out of bed and go to the gym. No one ever regrets a workout!

Humans are creatures of habit. When it comes to working out, doing the same routine repeatedly doesn't challenge your body. If you want to improve your health, you must change up the movements you do. A trainer can shake up your routine, so your body is regularly challenged and gives you the results you desire.

It's easy to see the correlation between a trainer and a financial advisor. An advisor or coach helps keep you accountable. Just like you would avoid skipping workouts with your trainer, you wouldn't want to tell your financial professional that you've gone deeper into debt. A financial advisor can also introduce you to investment products and new plans.

What a Financial Advisor Does

You've undoubtedly heard the term "financial advisor", but what does one actually do? A financial advisor will be a partner that helps you pursue your financial objectives and an educator on financial matters. While the average person can get bogged down in one area of their finances, an advisor sees the big picture.

Some activities with which a financial advisor will help:

1. Creating and sticking to a budget

2. Helping improve your credit score

3. Creating savings goals

4. Creating a plan to eliminate debt

5. Investing advice

6. Retirement planning

7. Insurance planning

8. Tax planning

9. Saving for college expenses

When to Hire a Financial Advisor

Unfortunately, just because you don't like dealing with financial issues doesn't mean you have to carte blanche to hand off the job to someone else. Advisors don't work for free. If you take this book seriously, handling your own financial planning really is not that overwhelming. But there are some situations that the average person just isn't equipped to handle.

You Have a Family or You're a Busy Professional

When you ask people what they wish they had more of, you'll generally get the same two answers: money and time. Hiring the right financial advisor can help you seek both.

When you have a career, a family, and a home to take care of, your finances can take a back seat. You don't want to make mistakes; however, you don't have the time to do the research necessary for making the best financial decisions for your family. Even if you do find the time to start delving into financial matters, it can be overwhelming (401[k]s, IRAs, ETFs, REITs). All the acronyms can seem like a foreign language. Within those acronyms, there are dozens of choices. It's like going into a grocery store with no shopping list and no recipe in mind. You're paralyzed by choice and indecision.

A financial advisor can help with this burden. They can give you information that you don't have time to find yourself, help you make tough decisions, and keep you on track to pursue your financial goals.

You're Self Employed

Being self-employed, carries many benefits, but also time-consuming challenges like payroll, adjusting business structure, healthcare, taxes, and retirement plans.

When you're busy trying to run and grow your business, this can be overwhelming. It can seem like a minefield since there are so many opportunities to make mistakes. Your decisions also affect your employees and their families.

A professional specializing in helping business owners can not only prevent you from making honest mistakes but can also uncover several advantages to owning a business. A professional might suggest restructuring as a limited liability company, which can have tax advantages and other incentives.

You Make a Lot of Money

As Biggie Smalls once said: *"Mo Money, Mo Problems"*. If you have a great deal of money to invest, it can be difficult to know how to prioritize those investments. Being in a high-tax bracket, your advisor needs to understand tax-saving strategies.

Your financial planner can help you properly allocate your money and advise you on ways to lower your tax burden.

You're High Net Worth

High net worth individuals have complicated financial decisions. They face unique challenges like multiple asset classes, estate and trust planning, and charitable endeavors. You want to ensure your assets are protected and accounted for if something tragic happens to you. There are financial planners who specialize in working with high net worth clients.

You're Getting Close to Retirement

Perhaps you've handled your financial planning on your own. As you get closer to retirement, you may want reassurance that you've handled matters properly. One of the largest financial fears is that we will outlive our money.

A financial planner can tell you if you're ready to retire. If you aren't, they will explain how to get ready, how and when to collect Social Security, and how to devise a strategy for withdrawing from your retirement/investment accounts.

Many "do it yourself" investors fail to plan for the fact is that their lives are finite. Most of my clients have a spouse that does not understand finances or doesn't care to understand finances. Sometimes while people are young and healthy, they take the path of least resistance and assume that they are invincible. What if that is not the case? What if the spouse who takes care of the finances passes away prematurely? What if you live to be 98 years old, do you want to be managing your money alone with no help? These are all questions that need to be addressed, but rarely are, because we don't like to talk about uncomfortable situations. The goal of a CERTIFIED FINANCIAL PLANNER™ Professional is to help through life's transitions and make sure both spouses are on the same page.

You Need a Neutral Third Party

I've given you some good ways that you and your spouse can handle your money. Having said this, sometimes two people are just not going to agree. Not only will they disagree, but they will be so far apart on the issue that no compromise is possible; a tough position for any couple to find themselves. Before you call a divorce lawyer, call a financial planner.

A financial planner isn't there to take sides. He or she will act as a neutral party who can advise a couple on the best way forward financially.

Finding an Ethical Advisor

Not all financial advisors are created equal and that doesn't mean how skilled they are at the job. An important distinction is whether your advisor is a fiduciary. A fiduciary is legally bound to give advice that is in the best interest of their client.

Unethical, non-fiduciary financial advisors might recommend financial products that are not suited for the investor. They do this to get paid a commission for selling them. That doesn't necessarily mean those financial products are bad, but not all products are best for everyone. All CERTIFIED FINANCIAL PLANNER™ Professionals are fiduciaries.

Not all advisors have the same education either. A CERTIFIED FINANCIAL PLANNER™ Professional has a college degree, at least three years (6,000 hours) of financial planning experience and has passed a comprehensive exam that requires years of study to get through. While the basic tenets of personal finance don't change (keep a budget, invest for retirement, and stay out of debt), the conditions that surround them do. You want an advisor who has current knowledge that is regularly updated. A

CFP® Professional must meet continuing education requirements.

Finding a CFP® Professional with a well-rounded education means they can offer clients valuable advice on investing, income taxation, retirement planning, employee benefits, estate planning, insurance, debt management, and every day financial issues.

The CFP® Board bestows the CERTIFIED FINANCIAL PLANNER™ designation and the board takes consumer complaints on its members. If an advisor is running afoul of the board, it can revoke a planner's credentials.

Several payment structures exist among financial advisors. Some are fee-based, some charge a flat rate per hour, some work on commission and others combine different payment models.

Before choosing a CFP® Professional, understand how their payment schedule works and choose a planner with a schedule with which you're comfortable.

Chapter Ten:

Redefining Retirement

The life span of humans is increasing. The average life expectancy in the U.S. is almost 79[16] and the average retirement age is 63[17]. The average person will spend sixteen years retired and much longer for those who plan to retire early. As we discussed earlier, individuals born in the 2000's are predicted to live past a hundred. Perhaps 16 years doesn't sound that long to be out of work, but have you ever been laid off and taken a few weeks to find another job?

At first, retirement is great. You can sleep as late as you want, check off items on your to-do list, or take a vacation. But without having something to do or somewhere you to be, you get bored quickly, especially true if your friends and family are still working. You're too young and healthy to sit in a rocking chair watching the world go by, so you must redefine retirement.

---

[16] *https://www.cdc.gov/nchs/fastats/life-expectancy.htm*

[17] *https://www.thebalance.com/average-retirement-age-in-the-united-states-2388864*

Deciding When to Retire

Arbitrarily picking an age to retire (or the "normal" age of 62 or 65) is not a retirement strategy. Several factors will come into play, including your health and financial status, as well as what your passion is. We will touch on those in a moment. Spending some time thinking about retiring before actually retiring is important. 'Why' you want to retire? A vague and uncomfortable thought process, but everyone should consider the 'why' because many who retire truly don't know their why.

Often, they've spent decades working in a career(s) and feel burnt out. The "working why" for someone may be to support their families, save for retirement, or because that's what you do when you become an adult.

The fallacy of retirement: You spend many decades working hard, saving money, and devoting your life to a career or a company. You hope that one day you can quit, not work anymore, and do what you want for the next two or three decades but have no plan. Let me tell you right now. That is a miserable existence! I know not because I have experienced it, but because I see countless clients do this. They do this because they are so tired of working that they can't do "it" anymore.

Boom! There "it" is. If you can't do "it" anymore, what can you do? What do you want to do? How can you further support your family? How can you make a positive impact on others? You must determine your "why" or "purpose" to have a fulfilling retirement.

My happiest clients had a clearly defined "retirement why": a purpose or something to look forward to during their retirement. Some of them have simple lives. Happy enough waking up at 6 a.m., climbing into their tractor, and baling hay on their East Tennessee farm. One client even has a pet cow that he dresses up for the holidays. Others travel all over. They are like trailblazers running off to see the Grand Canyon, Mount Rushmore, Alaska, Greece, Australia, and more. Other clients give back by spending time packing containers to send to Honduras or going on trips to serve orphanages. If you don't have your "retirement why", you are not ready to retire yet.

A large factor that may determine your time to retire is the state of your health. Hopefully, you won't face a health crisis that requires you to retire early. Many people are not ready to give up work but are forced to do so due to their health issues. This also carries an increase in medical expenses.

The second determinant is your financial situation. Earlier, we discussed your "retirement number". If have reached this point and no longer wish to work, you can retire. Getting a second opinion is never wrong. If you would like a second opinion, a financial advisor is the best person to consult.

If you plan to retire before age 65, you need some form of private healthcare. Medicare does not kick in until this age. If you've always had employer-sponsored health insurance, you may be in for a shocking surprise when you must pay your own.

What Do You Want Retirement to Look Like?

Just because you choose to retire does not mean you have to give up working entirely. You may choose to work part-time in your current industry on a consulting basis. Some even venture into totally different fields. Perhaps there is something you always wanted to do that you couldn't for whatever reason. Well, now you can do it. Maybe you would like to go back to school. Remember, college has no age limit.

Important considerations go into planning for your post-work life. If all your children are out of the house, you may choose to downsize to a smaller home. Perhaps after many years of yard work and maintenance, you don't want to be a homeowner. If you do not want to mow the grass and unclog the sink, you would probably consider moving into a condo or apartment.

Moving homes may not be enough; perhaps, you want to uproot completely. If you've always lived in the country, you might want to try city life. If you were tied to city life because of your career, you may want to retire to more rustic pastures. You might have heard about the high quality of life and low cost of living for expats in places like Panama and Costa Rica. Or perhaps you have grandchildren and want to move to be close to them.

Remember, you may have a spouse who needs to be consulted on this. Your spouse may not be ready to retire or pull up the stakes to move to a foreign country.

The point is having a plan in place can save you from feeling lost with thoughts such as, "Oh, I no longer have to go to work every day. What am I supposed to do?"

F.I.R.E Movement

F.I.R.E stands for Financial Independence, Retire Early. The concept is nothing new, but someone gave it a sleek acronym and a whole subculture was born.

Financial independence is something we all must define for ourselves. Broadly, it means you are not dependent on a job to pay living expenses. How can you manage that? To accomplish this one must have a few different means of providing passive income. This could mean investing, rental properties, being a silent partner in a successful business, or writing a book that provides royalties.

Retiring early within the F.I.R.E movement means retiring early. Early adopters of the plan were retired well before they turned 40. Many of them had good salaries, but they were not earning high-six figures by any means. They were able to retire early thanks to a combination of very frugal living and very smart investing.

With the right help, we can all accomplish smart investing. This needs to be coupled with the right level of frugality. The discipline required to follow this plan might not be appealing to everyone. Another characteristic many F.I.R.E acolytes have in common is that they do not have children. Having children is expensive and if you choose not to have any, that decision makes F.I.R.E much more realistic.

Plenty of those who are part of the F.I.R.E movement do continue some form of work after their early retirement. The movement isn't about not *wanting* to work; it's about not *having* to work.

What do F.I.R.Es do instead of punching a clock nine to five? Lots. They volunteer in their communities, run successful blogs, write books, create educational courses, or become public speakers advocating for the movement or become advocates for other needs.

I do realize this sounds a bit cult-like. You don't have to become immersed in the movement in order to be a part of it. However, it is a misnomer to think that early retirement means never working again.

Chapter Eleven:

Affording College

Good parents want what is best for their children. This often includes wanting them to get a college education, possibly with your financial help. However, college is not for everyone and paying for your child's education may be too detrimental to your own financial health.

College is Not for Everyone

The phrase "college isn't for everyone" used to mean "some people are too dumb for college." I believe our views have evolved on the topic. Just because someone is not well-suited for college doesn't mean they are unintelligent.

Classroom learning bores some folks. Others are poor test-takers no matter how well they understand the subject matter. Plenty of people simply don't like school and are ready to move on with their lives. If people know what they want to do and find jobs that allow them to support themselves and meet their financial goals, nothing is wrong with not attending college.

117

Some find a technical school or trade school more in line with what they desire to do with life.

People are pressured into attending college by parents, teachers, guidance counselors, and peers. This is a problem because college is not the best option for everyone. Those who succumb to the pressure, despite knowing that it's not a good path for them, may end up with tens of thousands of dollars in student loan debt. Some may have no degree to show for many hours spent in classrooms and find themselves deeply in debt. They feel they've let others down, as well as themselves, and feel guilty over the debacle.

You know your children better than anyone. Don't twist their arm to attend college if you know they are unlikely to do well. Do encourage them to explore what they'd like to do instead. Help them create a path that will allow them to be successful in whatever that might be.

There is More Than One Way

The traditional path to a college degree looks like this: apply to several colleges, attend the one that best suits you, borrow money to pay for it, attend for four years, and graduate at age twenty-two. This plan is not always workable, and many alternatives exist.

The cost of higher education is too high to make that path feasible for most people these days; however, more than one path to a college degree exists.

What did you want to do when you were eighteen? Maybe you weren't sure and spent a few semesters (and thousands of dollars) figuring it out. Perhaps you went to college, dropped out, and then came back. Time and money wasted because you started college before you were sure about what you wanted to do.

In many countries, high school graduates are encouraged to take a gap year. They take a whole year after graduation to work, travel, volunteer, and discover about what they are passionate. I wish students in the United States would adopt this practice. It would save the floundering that occurs when you're pushed into quickly deciding what you want to do with your life.

While it's important to help your children figure out what career path they want to take, finding out what they don't want to do is just as important. An extra year can go a long way in helping them figure out their future before they over-commit time and money.

If your children are college material, I strongly encourage them to complete some prerequisites at a local community college while living at home. Perhaps they could also work part-time. This can save thousands of dollars, not just in tuition expenses, but room-and-board too.

Once the prerequisites are completed, they can transfer to a more prestigious college. You need to make sure the credits transfer. This needs to be investigated before enrolling at the community college or university. They will still get the degree with the known college's name but will be able to graduate with much less (or no) debt.

No one is required to graduate in four years. Colleges accept students of all ages, not just 18-year-olds. Working full-time for a short period or part-time while in college can reduce student loan debt. It can help young people figure out what they do and don't like, which can help them choose a major when the time comes. Of course, when they do graduate, they would have a few years of work experience to add to their resumes. This can elevate them above their peers who graduated in four years and did not work.

Some employers offer tuition assistance as part of the benefits package or to retain/promote employees from within the company.

As I said, people can attend college at any age. Maybe your children don't want to go right after high school. They can always change their mind in a few years when they'll have some real-world experience. They may be better prepared to choose the right major, make good grades, and graduate.

Scholarships

When your child starts the junior year of high school, a full-time hobby should become researching scholarships. Many students are unaware that they have a good chance of receiving help if they seek it. Don't let them waste time going after the big fish. Many high-profile, big money scholarships have thousands of applicants. For the average student, these are too competitive. Many of these scholarships are for students with near-perfect grades. Not many of us had straight A's (or anywhere close to that) and our children do not either. There is nothing wrong with being an average student.

Instead, encourage them to find niche scholarships. If your child is not a 4.0 GPA type of student, not to worry. Many scholarships are rewarded for accolades other than grades. Financial aid is available for hobbies, talents, and skills that don't require straight A's.

Some of the offerings are quite humorous. You can receive help if you are vegetarian, a snowboarder, or interested in a career that will help further the potato industry. These are all real scholarships and they aren't exactly offering small potatoes. The vegetarian and potato communities are offering $5,000 and $10,000 a year, respectively.

Many of the lesser-known scholarships go unrewarded because no one applied for them. It can seem like a big job to apply for dozens of scholarships, but not all are asking for loads of documentation. Some only require an essay explaining why an applicant should be awarded the funds. These are often non-specific, generic essays, much like tweaking a cover letter for each job for which you apply. By making small changes for each entity awarding the scholarship, the applicant can use the same essay multiple times.

Some scholarships reward money for each term without having to go through the whole process each time. Others require the recipient to "re-up" each year.

I cannot express how significant these seemingly small scholarships are. The reward is quite high for work required.

Each dollar your child is awarded is a dollar not coming out of your pocket or one that isn't borrowed with interest.

It does pay, literally in this case, to be very organized when dealing with scholarships. They all have deadlines and different requirements. Once your child has found the scholarships they want, put them into a spreadsheet listing the requirements, due dates, and dollar amounts rewarded. Some will need references from faculty, family, sports coaches, music teachers, to name a few. These people may need a bit of encouragement to get their reference letter done on time.

I cannot emphasize enough how important it is to get scholarships to pay for college. Even if they are for small dollar amounts ($300 here and $500 there), it adds up. Remember how expensive textbooks are? Even if your child only wins enough to pay for textbooks, that's a help. If your child can graduate college without thousands in student loan debt, he or she will have a tremendous financial advantage when starting adult life. Applying for scholarships is not something you should encourage. It is something you should require.

First Thing's First

All parents would love to pay for their child's college education, especially if you have spent years paying off your own student loans. For many parents, the choice is between paying for a child's education and saving for their own retirement. A tough choice and parenthood is all about sacrifice; however, you must be realistic about your situation.

If you did spend years paying off your student loans, you may be behind when it comes to saving for retirement. If that's the case, time is not on your side. We talked about the power of compounding interest. For this to work, you need time. You do not have time, but your child does. Your child has more time to pay off student loans than you have to save for retirement.

This makes the choice clear. If you're behind on retirement saving, you need to prioritize this over paying for college. I've detailed several ways to make the cost of a college education less expensive. If your child chooses not to utilize any of those methods, that is not your fault.

Although this attitude may seem selfish, it's not. Think about how selfish it will feel to ask your adult children to borrow money or move in with them. This could easily happen if you do not plan.

529 Plans

This does not mean that you shouldn't invest in your child's education, but you should prioritize investing in your retirement. A 529 plan can be an ideal way to save for your child's education.

Two kinds of 529 plans:

The College Savings Plan is most common. Investments inside of the account seek growth and can be withdrawn tax-free for qualified education expenses. In 2017, the plan was expanded to include kindergarten through twelfth grade expenses. Most states have at least one 529 Plan, but you can choose a plan from any state. If another state has a plan with lower fees than your state, you should consider it. However, investing in an out-of-state plan causes you to lose the state tax deduction if that applies to you.

Prior to investing in a 529 plan, investors should consider whether the investor's or designated beneficiary's home state offers any state tax or other state benefits such as financial aid, scholarship funds, and protection from creditors that are only available for investments in such state's qualified tuition program. Withdrawals used for qualified expenses are federally tax-free. Tax treatment at the state level may vary. Please consult with your tax advisor before investing.

The second option is a 529 prepaid plan. This option allows you to prepay tuition for in-state public college, locking in the rate at the time of payment.

The owner of the 529 names a beneficiary, but you can change the beneficiary at any time if the child chooses not to go to college. Anyone can contribute to the plan, making it a nice way for family and friends to make monetary gifts. The contribution limits vary by state and go as high as $520,000. For tax purposes, the contributions are considered gifts. For 2019, gifts up to $15,000 qualify for the annual gift tax exclusion.

Most 529 Plans offer several investment options. These include static funds, bond funds, real estate funds, etc... You can mix-and-match the investments inside of your 529 plan to reach a certain asset allocation tailored to your level of risk tolerance.

What if your child does not go to college? You can change the beneficiary to another child or even yourself if you want a degree. This may be part of your retirement plan, getting a degree and embarking on a second career. If no one will be spending the money on education, withdrawn money will be subject to federal income taxes and a 10% penalty on the earnings. If the beneficiary gets a full college scholarship, the penalty for withdrawing the cash will be waived.

Chapter Twelve:

Estate Planning

An estate plan isn't just for wealthy people or those nearing retirement. If you have a family and assets, you need an estate plan. People often delay estate planning because they think they don't have enough assets to need one. They also don't know who to go to for guidance and don't like thinking about itemizing an estate. This is understandable.

Planning your estate means getting prepared for your death. People don't exactly relish thinking about death, especially their own. However, failing to create an estate plan can be devastating for the family left behind. If you do not have an estate plan in place, your state will create one for you. This complicates matters and your family will probably not like the complications.

If your name is on the title of your assets and you became incapacitated (physically or mentally) with no estate plan, only a court appointee can sign for you. That means a court, not your family, will determine how your assets are used via a conservatorship or guardianship.

If you die without an estate, your assets will be distributed under your state's probate laws. In many states, if you're married and have children, your spouse and children will each receive a portion of your estate. This may seem fine to you, but not all families are happy with it. Perhaps one or more of the children are estranged from the family. The money allocated to a spouse may not be enough to live on and the children might refuse to help. If you die and have minor children, the court will control their inheritance. Should both parents die while they have minor children, the court will determine the guardian.

What is an Estate Plan?

Your estate is made up of everything you own. This includes real estate, vehicles, bank accounts, investments, personal possessions, or life insurance; all material acquisitions that you can't take with you when you die.

You can't take it with you, but you can decide what happens to it. Whom do you want to receive the assets that make up your estate, what do you want them to receive, and when do you want them to receive them? An estate plan contains the answers to these questions.

A robust estate plan doesn't just determine where your assets go, but should also include:

1. Instructions to direct your care if you become disabled.

2. Name of a guardian and inheritance manager for your minor children.

3. Guidelines on providing for family members with special needs without disqualifying them from government benefits.

4. Guidelines on providing for family members who aren't responsible with money.

5. Information about life insurance, disability insurance, and long-term care insurance.

6. Minimized taxes, legal costs, and court costs.

7. Regular updates as your financial and familial situations change over the years.

Estate Planning Documents

An estate plan is an umbrella term for various documents. These are the documents that a complete estate plan should include.

Wills

A will details how your solely-owned property will be distributed after your death. It names a legal guardian for minor children and gives explicit funeral arrangements. Your will also names an executor; a person designated to manage the estate until all distributions are made.

Your will needs to be updated when you experience major life changes like getting married, divorced, or having children. It should also be updated when you experience a major change in your assets.

Wills are put into effect after death and go through a process called probate. A probate court oversees the administration of the will. They verify that the document is valid, and the deceased's property is distributed as instructed.

The probate process can take years, although that is out of the ordinary. The court charges a fee for this. That fee varies by state, but it's usually somewhere between 3% and 10% of the estate's value. If you're leaving behind a considerably large estate, those fees can amount to tens of thousands of dollars. Wills are also public record, which means anyone can read the contents. That's why most people with considerable assets set up a trust.

Trusts

A trust fund is a legal entity into which assets are placed to be managed by a trustee who acts as a neutral party. Once assets are put into a trust, you no longer own them. They become the property of the trust and are managed by the trustee. You are not required to put all your assets in the trust at the time you set it up.

You set conditions of the trust. You can stipulate that money from the trust can only be used for specific purposes. These stipulations could include education, age restrictions, or time-specific spending amounts. The funds from a trust can be measured out according to your specifications, whereas funds distributed in a will are given as a lump-sum payment.

The major advantage of a trust is that you are not subject to the probate process. This saves time and money while shielding your trust from public record.

Power of Attorney

To give someone power of attorney, you must sign a document that authorizes a designated person to make decisions and do what is needed on your behalf. Common uses are finance and medical decisions. A power of attorney is often used for elderly people who are unable to make decisions themselves. This is also useful for people who are outside of the country.

Without an established power of attorney, a guardian will be court-appointed to handle affairs you are unable to handle.

A Living Will

A living will is also known as an advanced healthcare directive. This is a document stating what, if any, medical measures you want to use in the event of something tragic. These are used for terminal illnesses, comas, or when one is in a permanent state of unconsciousness. A living will only goes into effect if you cannot communicate your own wishes.

Where to Go for Estate Planning

A CFP® Professional can help you understand the benefits of having an estate plan (and the negative consequences of not having one). They will explain some of the finer points, like the difference between a will and a trust.

Because the documents that make up an estate plan are legal, you will need to consult an attorney. You will want an attorney who specializes in this area. They are known as estate planning attorneys, estate law attorneys, or probate attorneys. These professionals will have a thorough understanding of the laws that govern how estates are inventoried, valued, dispersed, and taxed.

Your CFP® Professional may have an attorney on staff who can handle this or be able to recommend someone.

Chapter Thirteen:

Insurance

Most of us have "the big three" when it comes to insurance: homeowners, auto, and health. We have homeowners because our mortgage holder requires it, auto because the state requires it, and health because we don't want to go bankrupt over medical costs.

You may not be aware of other types of insurance policies that are just as important as "the big three."

Renter's Insurance

I am amazed at clients who rent an apartment/house and don't have renter's insurance. Some people believe that their landlord's insurance will cover a renter's belongings. This is incorrect. The insurance a landlord has on a rental property covers damage to the building, not the possessions of a tenant.

Some people do not think they need renter's insurance because they believe their belongings do not have much value. You may not have any Monet paintings, but imagine the cost of replacing everything you own. All your clothes, cookware, electronics, furniture, jewelry. This would cost thousands of dollars to replace it all, even if you're a dedicated minimalist.

For the sake of this argument, let's assume you do not have valuable items in your apartment. What you may not know is that renter's insurance covers much more than your belongings. It covers theft/vandalism inside and out of your apartment. It covers loss or accidental damage to your possessions. Most importantly, it provides personal liability coverage. If someone was injured in your home and that person sued you, you would be covered. This is also true if your pet were to hurt someone.

You might think you cannot afford renter's insurance, but it is very affordable. You can get a policy for less than $30 per month. Not having renter's insurance is a big mistake and could be a very costly one.

Life Insurance

If you have dependents, you need to have life insurance. If your parents co-signed your student loans, you should also have life insurance. I have heard terrible stories about adult children ending their lives partly due to their crippling amount of student loan debt. The loan services pressured their grieving parents who had co-signed the loans.

There are two basic types of life insurance policies: term and whole life.

Term life insurance: Term provides life insurance for a set number of years, usually twenty to thirty. If you die within that time frame, the policy pays out to your beneficiaries. Term life policies are less expensive than whole life because they have no cash value. A term policy is not worth anything unless the policyholder dies while the policy is in effect.

Whole life insurance: Whole provides coverage for the entirety of your life. Whole life is more expensive than term because it builds cash value. When you die, no matter when that happens, the policy pays out to your beneficiaries.

If you're taking the right financial steps, I generally recommend term life insurance. Hopefully, many changes will occur throughout the duration of your policy. Your children may be financially independent, or your home is paid off. Perhaps you have plenty of money saved for retirement and are planning to leave your career. If you were to die before those things happened, the policy would protect your family.

If you want to hedge your bets, you may like the idea of *guaranteed universal life insurance* (GUL). This is not the same as whole life, but it is designed to last your entire life. GUL doesn't build a cash value though, which makes it much less expensive than whole life. With a GUL policy, your monthly rates and coverage are guaranteed until the age of your choice, even past age 100.

I purchased a GUL for myself with a cost of about $475 per year and the policy is in effect until I reach age 100. If I pass away before age 100, my beneficiaries will collect a $100,000 payout. Basically, this worked out to be a 62-year term policy with a payout of $100,000. The maximum cost for me is $29,450. This can help my family pay for my burial and final expenses after I die. This is not the extent of my insurance planning, but rather just a part of how insurance plays a role in my financial plan.

Disability Insurance

Homeowners insurance protects your home and auto insurance protects your car. What does disability insurance protect? Likely your greatest asset is your ability to earn a living and provide for your family. Something well worth protecting, I'm sure you'll agree!

Disability insurance will replace part of your income if you are unable to work for an extended period due to illness or injury. When people think of a work-hindering situation, they often think of a catastrophic event or injury. A broken bone or a stubborn infection could mean missing a great deal of work. Could you absorb the loss of income? Even a fully funded emergency fund can be quickly depleted. If you earn a paycheck, you should have disability insurance.

Two kinds of disability insurance exist: short and long-term. Both types will replace a part of your income (up to a capped amount) if you become disabled. Some long-term policies will also cover job-retraining if you are unable to return to your previous career.

Some employers offer disability insurance and pay all or part of the premium. Some employers offer disability insurance as a voluntary benefit. This means you pay the entire premium, but it can be purchased via the employer's insurance broker at a discounted group rate. If your employer does not offer this, you can buy it privately from a broker or directly through an insurance company.

Both short and long-term disability insurance generally cost from 1% to 3% of your annual gross income.

Long-Term Care Insurance

Long-term care insurance is not something young people think about and most do not need it. As we age into our fifties and sixties, long-term care becomes more important. If you are younger than fifty, you should be speaking with your parents about how they've planned for late in life. These decisions will affect the whole family. More than 34 million Americans[18] have provided unpaid care to an adult over the age of fifty in the past twelve months. Many of these people fall into what is termed "the sandwich generation." These are people who care for their aging parents (or another family member) while also caring for their children. Watching an elderly parent isn't an ideal situation for most people. If your parents live far from you, it will be impossible unless one of you is willing to uproot and move.

Long-term care insurance covers assistance with day-to-day tasks like bathing, dressing, and getting out of bed. They will pay

---

[18] https://www.caregiver.org/caregiver-statistics-demographics

for this type of care in your home, a nursing home, an assisted care home, or an adult care day program.

If you're foregoing long-term care insurance because you have health insurance or think Medicare will cover it, you're making a mistake. Your regular health insurance does not cover long-term care. Medicare only covers short stays in a nursing home and a limited amount of in-home care.

Waiting too long to buy this insurance may mean you're no longer eligible. If you already have a debilitating condition, you won't qualify for coverage. If this happens, you will be out-of-pocket for these expenses. I don't think I have to tell you how expensive health care in America is. The only program that could come to your aid in this situation is Medicaid, but that requires you to have exhausted nearly all your savings.

Some employers offer the option to buy long-term care insurance at a group rate from the company's broker. One can also buy it privately. Costs are determined by factors such as your age, health, gender, and marital status. A rough estimate of the cost for long-term care, if you are in your mid-fifties, is $2,000 to $3,000 per year. This is a drop in the bucket compared to paying out-of-pocket.

Chapter Fourteen:

Enjoy It

You might be surprised that I've included a chapter on enjoying your money. I'm a CERTIFIED FINANCIAL PLANNER® Professional after all. Shouldn't I be telling you to save every penny? I'm not going to tell you to save every penny because life is for living.

Too Frugal

There is nothing wrong with being frugal. It's an admirable trait and more people should think along those lines. But one can be obsessed with saving and become too frugal. More accurately, there is a big difference between being frugal and being cheap or stingy.

Frugal people do not try to pay the least amount of money for everything they buy; rather they want to get the most for their money. Frugal people aren't stingy with their money, but they do not waste it.

Being cheap (in a bad way) often costs you more money in the long run. If you buy the cheapest vacuum cleaner available, even though you have two dogs and three cats, that vacuum will not last very long. You'll have to buy a replacement vacuum much sooner than if you had done research to find the best vacuums for homes with pets. Or you could have saved up enough money to buy a better vacuum. Not only is this aggravating, but you are also without a working vacuum and must spend more money buying a new one.

Being cheap can also mean missing out. If you are the person who insists on dividing up the dinner check down to the penny, you will not get many dinner invitations. Sure, if some of the people at the table ordered several drinks, it's unfair to split the check evenly. But if someone ordered a meal that was a few dollars more than yours, let it go. It's not only cheap, but some people will see it as downright rude.

Let's say your close friend is having a destination wedding. You're invited but you're also worried about the cost. If you turn down the invitation for this reason, your friend will be hurt, and you have excluded yourself from an exciting event. And for what? Money, just money. It's not that you are unable to afford it, you're just too cheap. Of course, some people may actually be unable to pay, but make sure to budget ahead for expenses like these.

No one should fritter away money, no matter how much of it they have. You work hard for your money, and you should get the most out of the money you spend. That's what being frugal means. So, loosen the purse strings every now and then.

You Work Hard for Your Money and Are Allowed to Enjoy It

Some people cannot bear to spend money due to past events in their lives. Perhaps they grew up during the Depression, in an impoverished family, or had neglectful parents. These circumstances can have a profound effect on how we think about and spend money. For some people, the feeling of being poor never goes away, no matter how much money they have. Even too much can feel like not enough.

Some people are afraid to spend money because they fear bankruptcy from a health issue. This is not an unreasonable fear. Medical bills are a leading cause of bankruptcy. You can help insulate yourself from this possibility by having the right types and adequate amounts of insurance.

Let's be honest. If a medical catastrophe does happen, the small amount you saved by cleaning your own home or not taking your dream trip won't make a huge difference. For most people, only insurance can cover massive medical bills no matter how well you have saved.

Saving and never spending is a sad way to live. You work hard for your money. You should use some of your money on what you enjoy or on items that make your life better. Just make sure you hold an emergency fund, stick to a monthly budget, save for retirement, and save for your children's future.

You and your spouse both work full time. Why are you spending your weekends cleaning the house and doing yard work unless you enjoy them? You can hire a service to do this and give yourselves more free time to spend together doing things you do enjoy.

The day will come when you can't physically accomplish trips such as hiking the Appalachian Trail or taking a long flight abroad. You can't buy back time no matter how much money you have saved.

You Can Buy Happiness

As a frugal person, you want to get the most for your money. In this case, you want the most happiness for your money. What can you buy that will make you happy? Nothing, you might think, because we've always been told that money doesn't buy happiness. But it can. You just have to know what to buy.

That's a bit disingenuous of me. For the most part, buying things won't make you happy. But spending money can. There are two ways you can spend your money to make you happy. Spending on experiences and on others can bring you joy.

What is the last big-ticket item you bought? Maybe a television, a laptop, or a piece of jewelry. Do you feel excited by that item, think back fondly on the day you acquired it, tell people about it, show them pictures of it? Did you and a close friend or partner buy this together?

Likely you answered "no" to all these questions. Now think back to the last big-ticket experience you bought. Maybe an expensive dinner, tickets to a concert/play, or a vacation. Now ask yourself the same questions about this experience. You likely answered "yes" to all those questions. That exercise shows exactly why we are happier when we spend money on experiences rather than on the acquisition of more "stuff."

You might argue that worldly possessions make you happy because you use them often. But that's just it. You use them each day and they blend into a part of everyday life. If we had Christmas every day, it would no longer be special.

That isn't to say those items we use every day cannot enhance our lives. Anyone who has ever replaced an old, saggy mattress with a brand new one knows this. Material products that enhance your life such as a good mattress, a reliable car, a good set of kitchen knives, are good uses of money. They won't make us happy in the way experiences will, but they can make life easier.

The other way you can use your money to buy happiness for yourself is to spend it on others. It doesn't have to be an extravagant charitable gesture or flashy gift. It's not the amount you spend that makes you happy. Spending money on other people gives us the satisfaction that we have helped our fellow human beings. You can get this happiness boost with small gestures. This could include buying your co-worker a cup of coffee or buying an extra bag of pet food to donate to a local animal shelter. Seeing other people happy can make us happy.

There is a Ceiling

If I asked you how much money you needed each year to be happy, what number would you give me? Maybe six-figures or even a million dollars?

It turns out that the price of "optimal emotional well-being" is around $75,000[19] per year. These are the numbers we need to achieve "positive emotions on a day-to-day basis". I think this would be pretty satisfying to most of us. Of course, the cost of living is different in each area, but you get the point. When we reach $95,000[20], we are making the ideal amount to conduct a "life evaluation." This accounts for things like long-term goals, peer comparisons, and other macro-level metrics.

This might be more than some of us make, but there are two important ideas to gather from these studies. One, the salary needed to "be happy" is not as high as most of us probably suspected. Two, it is possible to make too much money when it comes to happiness. A study found that there is a decline in emotional well-being and life satisfaction after $95,000. Researchers believe that incomes beyond this number can lead to unhealthy social comparisons and unfulfilling material pursuits.

I am not encouraging you to turn down any raises to stay below the $95,000 "happiness" threshold. It simply means that pursuing more money isn't going to make you happier once you

---

[19] http://content.time.com/time/magazine/article/0,9171,2019628,00.html

[20] http://money.com/money/5157625/ideal-income-study/

reach that level. You can be happier by achieving career goals unrelated to salary such as being promoted or being assigned to new projects. Now you have seen how you can use money to buy happiness in your personal life.

Conclusion

"To be in hell is to drift; to be in heaven is to steer." While this George Bernard Shaw quote can be applied to many areas of life, perhaps nowhere is it truer than when it comes to issues around personal finance.

Money is without question a central issue in everyone's life. We need money to pay our bills, take care of our families, to educate our children, to support our communities, to reach our goals, and to fund our retirement. But none of us want to think about money all the time. We'd rather spend time on the other things that matter; our families, friends, careers, and hobbies.

My hope and desire with this adventure is to use my education, expertise, and experience in personal finance to provide you two key takeaways. The first is roots to keep you grounded in the investment and financial decisions you make and wings so that you can freely pursue the passions you value most.

About the Author

Jonathan P. Bednar, II, CFP® was born in Jonesboro, Arkansas and grew up in Little Rock, Arkansas. He graduated from the Sam Walton College of Business, University of Arkansas, in May 2009 with a B.S.B.A. in Finance. He completed us CERTIFIED FINANICAL PLANNER™ certification course work through the University of Georgia and became a CERTIFIED FINANCIAL PLANNER™ Professional in 2018.

Jonathan is co-owner of Paradigm Wealth Partners in Knoxville, TN. He partners with his father, Jon P. Bednar, as a Wealth Advisor. Jonathan enjoys guiding his clients to make informed financial decisions using financial planning as a means to solve their investment and retirement decisions. Jonathan has been quoted in articles seen in Forbes.com, Bankrate.com, Realtor.com, and other publications

In August 2014, Jonathan married his wife Becky who is a commercial banker. In March of 2017 they welcomed their first child, Cate, into their family. Cate is referred "Paradigm Princess" around the office.

Jonathan specializes in helping families and professionals pursue their financial goals free from anxiety around money. He often provides guidance for clients with investment planning, education planning, employer benefits, and retirement planning.

Feedback

If you enjoyed this book and think it can have an impact on others please provide feedback.

Resources

You can find resources and PDFs in the "Financial Toolkit" section of the website

www.ParadigmWealthPartners.com.

Some of the PDFs you will find is:

Document Locator
SMART Goals Worksheet
Annuity Review Checklist
Budget Worksheet
Dave Ramsey's 7 Baby Steps
What Keeps You Up at Night?

Made in the USA
Columbia, SC
28 October 2020